uCertify Guide for EC-Council Exam 312-49

Computer Hacking forensic Investigator

Pass your CHFI Certification in first attempt

uCertify Team
www.ucertify.com

Copyright

uCertify Guide for EC-Council Exam 312-49

Foreword

IT certification exams require a lot of study and practice. Many of our customers spend weeks, if not months preparing for the exam. While most classroom training and certification preparation software do a good job of covering exam material and providing practice questions, summarization of the highlights and key study points is often missing.

This book is intended to bridge the gap between preparation and the final exam. It is designed to be an easy reference that will walk you through all the exam objectives with easy to remember key points required to successfully pass the certification exam. It reinforces the key points, while helping you focus on the exam requirements. The benefits are multifold and can help you save hours of exam review, while keeping key concepts fresh in your mind before the exam. This critical review will help you with the final exam preparation touches and give you the confidence needed for the big day.

Benefits of this exam countdown and quick review guide:

1.Focused approach to reviewing exam material – review what you must know.

2.All key exam concepts highlighted and reinforced.

3.Time saving – must know facts at your finger tips in one condensed version.

4. Detailed explanations of all possible answers to practice questions to ensure your grasp of the topic.

5 A full length simulation exam to determine your exam readiness.

Table of Contents

6

How this book will help you

uCertify's guide for EC-Council Exam 312-49 is an invaluable supplement to those in the final stages of their preparation for the EC-Council 312-49Computer Hacking Forensic Investigator.

This book is organized into three sections.

Section A

Section A contains general information about the book and Exam 312-49. It describes the exam objectives, pre-requisites, exam format, test taking tips and strategies and more.

Section B

Section B contains eleven chapters. Each chapter contains a Quick Review of the material you need to know for a given objective. It reinforces concepts reviewed via pop Pop Quiz and practice questions.

- **Pop Quiz** - Short, to-the-point questions with definitive answers.

- **Practice Questions** - At the end of each chapter, a series of questions test your understanding of the topics covered in the chapter. These questions are patterned after actual exam questions and difficulty levels. Detailed explanations are provided for each question, explaining not just the correct answer, but the incorrect answers as well, to ensure a real grasp of the question.

Section C

Section C contains fifty-five full-length questions. These questions will test your preparation for the exam within a stipulated period. The Answer Sheet for the exam contains a complete analysis of the question.

Finally, the Appendices includes Acronyms and Glossary followed by References and Index. This is very handy for last minute reviews.

We wish you all the best on your exam!

Principal contributors:

Adarsh Srivastava,

Betsy Rivers,

Prashant Gupta,

uCertify Team

Section A

Introduction

About uCertify

uCertify is a leading provider of IT certification exam preparation software. For over a decade, we have been preparing top quality preparation guides for over 200 IT certification exams. Our software Preparation Kits (Prepkits, as we call them), contain exhaustive study material, tips, study notes and hundreds of practice questions that culminate in a full length simulated preparation exam. Choose exams from vendors such as Microsoft, Oracle, CompTIA, SUN, CIW, EC-Council, ADOBE, CISCO, ITIL, IBM, LPI, and ISC-2. Authored by highly experienced and certified professionals, uCertify PrepKits not only guarantee your success at getting certified, but also equip you to truly understand the subject.

As they say, "Successful people don't do different things, they do things differently." uCertify's preparation methodology is that difference. We will give you a competitive edge over others who may be paper certified but not qualified to use the skills on the job. A customer pass rate of over 99%, is testimony to the success of our methodology. We guarantee it! Our industry best 100% money back guarantee is second to none! Check it out at:

http://www.ucertify.com/about/guarantee.html

Learn more about us at www.ucertify.com and www.prepengine.com , our smarter learning platform, which powers each of our Prepkits.

About this Book

What this book is and what it's not

This book is invaluable as a final review guide for EC-Council Exam 312-49. It is a supplement to your exam preparation, be it classroom training, practical experience, or even test preparation software. The book is designed to help you save time while ensuring your are ready, by providing you a Quick Review of all exam objectives, without having to review all exam material. In addition, the book helps reinforce key concepts and terminology, both of which are important to review just before your exam. A big bonus is the full length exam simulation practice test that will be a good indicator of your exam readiness.

This book is not a substitute for exhaustive test preparation services such as uCertify Prepkits or classroom training. uCertify strongly recommends that you first study the exam material extensively and gain as much practical experience as possible in the areas you are expected to have skills in. Use this book as a final review before your actual exam.

About Exam 312-49: Computer Hacking Forensic Investigator

EC-Council's 312-49 exam recognizes the knowledge and skills of a candidate to identify, track, and prosecute cyber-criminals. It also recognizes the knowledge of detecting hacking attacks and properly extracting evidence to report the crime and conduct audits to prevent future attacks. It deals with the various possible applications and methods of cyber crime. The computer hacking forensic investigator exam provides knowledge about preparation and application of forensic methods in electronic media.

Benefits of Certification

IT certification is an industry wide, internationally standardized, highly recognized method that demonstrates your technical problem skills and expertise in a given area. By passing a certification exam, an individual shows to his current or potential employer that s/he recognizes the value of staying current with the latest technology. The certification process helps you gain market relevant skills culminating in an industry respected certificate in one or more areas offered for certification. While not all employers require certification, getting certified is tangible proof of your motivation and skills as an IT professional. Surveys consistently show certified professionals to earn more than their counterparts who do not have a formal certification. Most certified professional have found that their financial investment in training and certification is paid off by gains in salary, job opportunities, or expanded roles, typically over a short period of time.

Exam Registration

EC-Council exams can be registered and taken at Prometric testing centers across the globe. Be sure to give yourself plenty of time to prepare for the exam before you schedule your exam day.

Name	Phone (US and Canada)	Phone Other Countries
Prometric: http://www.prometric.com	1-800-775-3926	1-410-843-8000

Exam Objectives & Skills Expected

EC-Council has specified more than forty three objectives for the exam 312-49. These objectives are grouped under eleven topics. Candidates for the 312-49 certification exam are expected to be competent in the following areas:

- Understanding Internet laws.

- Reviewing CSIRT and computer forensic lab.

- Understanding file system, hard disk, and digital media devices, Windows, Linux and Macintosh boot process.

- Using Windows and Linux forensic tools.

- Identifying methods of investigating using Encase.

- Understanding data acquisition and duplication.

- Understanding partition recovery tools and methods.

- Performing steganography.

- Deploying password cracking tools and attacks.

- Learning network forensics.

- Understanding wireless and Web attacks.

- Identifying types of DoS attacks.

- Studying E-Mail sending-receiving System.

- Understanding corporate espionage.

- Reviewing laws of Copyright and Trademark.

- Reviewing laws on sexual harassment.

- Identifying effects, prevention, and laws of child pornography.

- Understanding features and tools for PDA forensics.

- Understanding features and tools for ipod forensics.

- Understanding working and functions of Blackberry.

- Creating investigative reports.

Who should take this exam?

The EC-Council Certified Computer Hacking Forensic Investigator (CHFI) is appropriate for you if you are working or want to work in a typically complex computing environment of medium-to-large organizations. There are no specific prerequisites for this test, although it is recommended that you should take the CEH Exam before enrolling into CHFI program. However, it is not mandatory to pass the CEH exam before applying for the CHFI exam.

FAQ for EC-Council Exam 312-49

Q. What are the pre-requisites to take the 312-49 exam?

A. There are no prerequisites for writing the Hacking Forensic Investigator (CHFI) 312-49 exam, although it is recommended that you should take the CEH Exam before enrolling into CHFI program. However, it is not mandatory to pass the CEH exam before applying for the CHFI exam.

Q. What is the format of the exam?

A. This exam consists of Multiple Choice, Hot Area, Drag and Drop, Build list and reorder, and Build a Tree questions. The exam may be adaptive, and simulation type of questions may also be asked. There are no Case study type questions for this exam.

Q. What does one gain from this certification?

A. EC-Council's 312-49 test is designed to measure your ability to recognize the knowledge and skills of a candidate to identify, track, and prosecute cyber-criminals. It also recognizes the knowledge of detecting hacking attacks and properly extracting evidence to report the crime and conduct audits to prevent future attacks. By passing the test 312-49: Computer Hacking Forensic Investigator, you will be provided by the CHFI certification.

Q. How many questions are asked in the exam?

A. You will be required to attempt approximately 50 questions.

Q. What is the duration of the exam?

A. Users are required to attempt all questions within 120 minutes.

Q. What is the passing score?

A. You need a score of 700 out of 1000 to pass the exam.

Q. What is the exam retake policy?

A. There is no restriction on the number of times a candidate can appear for the examination. There is no waiting period between attempts.

Q. Where can I get more practice questions?

A. Donwload uCertify PrepKit to have more Practice questions from the donwload link below:

http://www.ucertify.com/exams/EC-Council/312-49.html

Q. Where can the test 312-49 be taken?

A. EC-Council exams may be taken at Prometric testing facilities.

Q. What is the exam fee?

A. The net price for taking test 312-49 is US$250. The net price does not include applicable taxes, vouchers, promotions or membership discounts you may have.

Test Taking Tips

- Stay calm and relaxed.

- When you start the test, read the question and ALL its options carefully even if you think you know the answer. Be prepared for tricky questions!

- If you are taking an adaptive test, remember that you will not get a chance to change your answer once you move on, so be sure before you mark the answer. In a linear test you will have a chance to change the answer before you hand in the exam.

- If you know the correct answer, attempt the question and move on. If you are not sure, mark your best guess and move on. If it is a linear test, you should also bookmark the question so that you can return to it later.

- Sometimes related questions help you get the right answers for the questions you were unsure of, so it is always a good idea to bookmark the question.

- If you are unsure of the correct answer, read all the options and eliminate the options that are obviously wrong. Then choose from the options left.

- Once you have finished answering all the questions, check the time left. If you have time, review the book marked questions.

- Never leave a question unanswered. All certification tests that we know are timed and count unanswered questions as wrong. If you don't have time, take a blind guess.

Before the test

- Be confident and relaxed.

- Sleep well the night before the exam.

The Big Day

It is strongly recommended that you arrive at the testing center at least 15 minutes before the exam is scheduled. Don't forget to bring two pieces of identification with you, one of which must be a photo I.D., such as a valid driver's license. You will be required to show the identification when you sign in at the testing center. The center-in-charge will explain the examination rules, after which you will be asked to sign a document that states that you fully understand and abide by the rules of the exam.

Once you are signed in, you will be directed to the exam room. Carrying anything into the room is strictly prohibited. You will be given a few blank pieces of paper and a pen upon entering the room. Once you complete the exam, your score will be tabulated and you will know immediately if you have passed or failed the exam. If you failed, you can retake it as soon as you are ready, even the same day. It is a good idea to note down all the difficult topics you faced during the exam and revise this review guide or other training material before retaking the exam. If you fail the same exam a second time, you must wait at least 14 days before you will be allowed to reschedule.

The testing center-in-charge is typically available to assist with administrative aspects of the testing.

Section B

Core Contents

Chapter 1 - Law and Computer Forensics

Overview

Cyber law is a very wide term, which wraps up the legal issue related to use of communicative, transactional, and distributive aspect of networked information device and technologies. It is commonly known as INTERNET LAW. These laws are important to apply, as Internet does not tend to make any geographical and jurisdictional boundaries clear; this is the reason why Cyber law is not very efficient. A single transaction may involve the laws of at least three jurisdictions:

1. The laws of the state/nation in which the user resides.

2. The laws of the state/nation that apply where the server hosting the transaction is located.

3. The laws of the state/nation, which apply to the person or business with whom the transaction takes place.

Real individuals connect to the Internet and interact with others; it is possible for them to withhold personal information and make their real identities anonymous. If there are laws that could govern the Internet, then it appears that such laws would be fundamentally different from laws that geographic nations use today.

Cyber crime is an unlawful act in which a computer is either a tool or a target or both to harm an individual, organization, or any free body. It involves theft, fraud, forgery, etc. done using the Internet.

Cyber Crime falls in the following two categories:

1. The computer as a target: Using a computer to attack other computers.

2. The computer as a weapon: Using a computer to commit real world crime.

Cyber laws came into existence in the early 90's. They were formulated to prevent the growing chaos and crime in cyber space. The laws of a nation may have extraterritorial impact extending the jurisdiction beyond the sovereign and territorial limits of that nation. This is particularly problematic as the medium of the Internet does not explicitly recognize sovereignty and territorial limitations. There is no uniform, international jurisdictional law of universal application, and such questions are generally a matter of conflict of laws, particularly private international law. An example would be where the contents of a Web site are legal in one country and illegal in another. In the absence of a uniform jurisdictional code, legal practitioners are generally left with a conflict of law issue.

Another major problem of cyberlaw lies in whether to treat the Internet as if it were physical space (and thus subject to a given jurisdiction's laws) or to act as if the Internet is a world unto itself (and therefore free of such restraints). Those who favor the latter view often feel that government should leave the Internet community to self-regulate.

Key Points

Internet Laws

- Cyberstalking is the use of the Internet or other electronic means to stalk someone. It has been defined as the use of information and communications technology, particularly the Internet, by an individual or group of individuals, to harass another individual, group of individuals, or organization. The behavior includes false accusations, monitoring, the transmission of threats, identity theft, damage to data or equipment, the solicitation of minors for sexual purposes, and gathering information for harassment purposes.

- The Equal Credit Opportunity Act (ECOA) is a United States law (codified at 15 U.S.C. 1691 et seq.), enacted in 1974, that makes it unlawful for any creditor to discriminate against any applicant, with respect to any aspect of a credit transaction, on the basis of race, color, religion, national origin, sex, marital status, or age; to the fact that all or part of the applicant's income derives from a public assistance program; or to the fact that the applicant has in good faith exercised any right under the Consumer Credit Protection Act. The law applies to any person who, in the ordinary course of business, regularly participates in a credit decision, including banks, retailers, bankcard companies, finance companies, and credit unions.

- The Electronic Communications Privacy Act of 1986 (ECPA Pub. L. 99-508, Oct. 21, 1986, 100 Stat. 1848, 18 U.S.C. 2510) was enacted by the United States Congress to extend government restrictions on wire taps from telephone calls to include transmissions of electronic data by computer. Specifically, ECPA was an amendment to Title III of the Omnibus Crime Control and Safe Streets Act of 1968 (the Wiretap Statute), which was primarily designed to prevent unauthorized government access to private electronic communications. The ECPA also added new provisions prohibiting access to stored electronic communications, i.e., the Stored Communications Act,18 U.S.C. 2701-2712.

- The Privacy Act of 1974, 5 U.S.C. 552a, establishes a code of fair information practice that governs the collection, maintenance, use, and dissemination of personally identifiable information about individuals that is maintained in systems of records by federal agencies. A system of records is a group of records under the control of an agency from which information is retrieved by the name of the individual or by some identifier assigned to the individual. The Privacy Act requires that agencies give the public notice of their systems of records by publication in the Federal Register. The Privacy Act prohibits the disclosure of information from a system of records of the subject individual, unless the disclosure is pursuant to one of twelve statutory exceptions.

- The Fair Credit Reporting Act (FCRA) is an American federal law (codified at 15 U.S.C. 1681 et seq.) that regulates the collection, dissemination, and use of consumer information, including consumer credit information. Along with the Fair Debt Collection Practices Act (FDCPA), it forms the base of consumer credit rights in the United States. It was originally passed in 1970, and is enforced by the US Federal Trade Commission.

- The CAN-SPAM Act of 2003 establishes the United States' first national standards for the sending of commercial e-mail and requires the Federal Trade Commission (FTC) to enforce its provisions. The acronym CAN-SPAM derives from the bill's full name: Controlling the Assault of Non-Solicited Pornography And Marketing Act of 2003. This is also a play on the usual term for unsolicited email of this type, spam. The bill was sponsored in Congress by Senators Conrad Burns and Ron Wyden.

Pop Quiz

Q1: Which U.S.C. laws governs the fraudulent activities associated with computers?

Ans: 18 U.S.C. 1030

Q2: Which US laws makes it unlawful for any creditor to discriminate against any applicant, on the basis of race, color, religion, national origin, sex, marital status, or age?

Ans: The Equal Credit Opportunity Act

- The CAN-SPAM Act is commonly referred to as the "You-Can-Spam" Act because the bill explicitly legalizes most e-mail spam. In particular, it does not require e-mailers to get permission before they send marketing messages. It also prevents states from enacting stronger anti-spam protections, and prohibits individuals who receive spam from suing spammers. The Act has been largely un-enforced, despite a letter to the FTC from Senator Burns, who noted that "Enforcement is key regarding the CAN-SPAM legislation."

- Federal law 18 U.S.C. 2510 is related to wire, oral, and electronic communication.

- 18 U.S.C. 1029 is related to fraudulent activity associated with access drives, and 18 U.S.C. 1030 is related to fraudulent activity associated with computers.

- Federal law 18 U.S.C. 1028 deals with fraud related to possession of false identification documents.

- Malicious Communications Act (1998) in the United Kingdom, classified cyber stalking as a criminal offense.

- Stalking by Electronic Communications Act (2001) is formed in Texas to prevent cyber stalking.

- Anti-Cyber-Stalking law is the first U.S. cyber stalking law went into effect in 1999 in California. Other states include prohibition against cyber stalking in their harassment or stalking legislation.

- Federal law 18 U.S.C. 2510 is related to wire, oral, and electronic communication. 18 U.S.C. 1029 is related to fraudulent activity associated with access drives, and 18 U.S.C. 1030 is related to fraudulent activity associated with computers.

- In the local network security test, the security testing team simulates as an employee or other person with an authorized connection to the organization's network.

- The credit card issuing company violates the Privacy law if a company is providing their customer's financial and personal details to other companies.

Key Terms

ECOA	Equal Credit Opportunity Act
ECPA	Electronic Communications Privacy Act
FCRA	Fair Credit Reporting Act
OSI	Open Systems Interconnection

Test Your Knowledge

Q1. John works as a professional Ethical Hacker. He is assigned a project to test the security of www.we-are-secure.com. He is working on the Linux operating system. He wants to sniff the we-are-secure network and intercept a conversation between two employees of the company through session hijacking. Which of the following tools will John use to accomplish the task?

    A.   Hunt

    B.   Ethercap

    C.   IPChains

    D.   Tripwire

Q2. John works as a Network Security Professional. He is assigned a project to test the security of www.we-are-secure.com. He is working on the Linux operating system and wants to install an Intrusion Detection System on the We-are-secure server so that he can receive alerts about any hacking attempts. Which of the following tools can John use to accomplish the task?

Each correct answer represents a complete solution. Choose all that apply.

    A.   Tripwire

    B.   Snort

    C.   Samhain

    D.   SARA

Q3. Which of the following is used to authenticate asymmetric keys?

    A.   Demilitarized zone (DMZ)

    B.   Digital signature

    C.   Password

    D.   MAC Address

Q4.   Which of the following components are usually found in an Intrusion detection system (IDS)?

Each correct answer represents a complete solution. Choose two.

A.   Sensor

B.   Firewall

C   Console

D.   Modem

E.   Gateway

Q5.   In which of the following access control models can a user not grant permissions to other users to see a copy of an object marked as secret that he has received, unless they have the appropriate permissions?

A.   Mandatory Access Control (MAC)

B.   Role Based Access Control (RBAC)

C.   Discretionary Access Control (DAC)

D.   Access Control List (ACL)

Answer Explanation

A1.   Answer option A is correct.

In such a scenario, John will use Hunt which is capable of performing both the hacking techniques, sniffing and session hijacking.

Answer option B is incorrect. Ethercap is a network sniffer and packet generator. It may be an option, but John wants to do session hijacking as well. Hence, he will not use Ethercap.

Answer option C is incorrect. IPChains is a firewall.

Answer option D is incorrect. Tripwire is a file and directory integrity checker.

A2.   Answer options B and C are correct.

In such a situation, John can use either the Snort or Samhain tool as an Intrusion Detection System.

Answer options A and D are incorrect. Tripwire is a file and directory integrity checker. Security Auditor's Research Assistant (SARA) is a third generation Unix-based security analysis tool that supports the FBI Top 20 Consensus on Security. It is an upgrade of the SATAN tool and operates on most UNIX platforms. SARA interfaces with NMAP for OS fingerprinting. The main features of SARA are as follows:

It is integrated with National Vulnerability Database.

It supports CVE standards.

It performs SQL injection tests.

It is available as a free-use open SATAN-oriented license.

A3.   Answer option B is correct.

A digital signature is used to authenticate asymmetric keys.

Digital signature is a message signed with a sender's private key can be verified by anyone who has access to the sender's public key, thereby proving that the sender signed it and that the message has not been tampered with. This is used to ensure authenticity.

Public-key cryptography, also known as asymmetric cryptography, is a form of cryptography in which the key used to encrypt a message differs from the key used to decrypt it.

Answer option A is incorrect. Demilitarized zone (DMZ) or perimeter network is a small network that lies in between the Internet and a private network. It is the boundary between the Internet and an internal network, usually a combination of firewalls and bastion hosts that are gateways between inside networks and outside networks. DMZ provides a large enterprise network or corporate network the ability to use the Internet while still maintaining its security.

Answer options C and D are incorrect. Password and MAC address are not used to authenticate asymmetric keys.

A4.   Answer options A and C are correct.

An Intrusion detection system (IDS) is used to detect unauthorized attempts to access and manipulate computer systems locally or through the Internet or an intranet. It can detect several types of attacks and malicious behaviors that can compromise the security of a network and computers. This includes network attacks against vulnerable services, unauthorized logins and access to sensitive data, and malware (e.g. viruses, worms, etc.). An IDS also detects attacks that originate from within a system. In most cases, an IDS has three main components: Sensors, Console, and Engine. Sensors generate security events. A console is used to alert and control sensors and to monitor events. An engine is used to record events and to generate security alerts based on received security events. In many IDS implementations, these three components are combined into a single device. Basically, following two types of IDS are used :

- Network-based IDS

- Host-based IDS

The following components are usually found in an Intrusion detection system (IDS):

- Sensor

- Console

Answer options B, D, and E are incorrect. A firewall, modem, and gateway are usually not found in an Intrusion detection system (IDS).

A5.   Answer option A is correct.

Mandatory Access Control (MAC) is a model that uses a predefined set of access privileges for an object of the system. Access to an object is restricted on the basis of the sensitivity of the object and granted through authorization. Sensitivity of an object is defined by the label assigned to it. For example, if a user receives a copy of an object that is marked as "secret", he cannot grant permission to other users to see this object unless they have the appropriate permission.

Answer option B is incorrect. Role-based access control (RBAC) is an access control model. In this model, a user can access resources according to his role in the organization. For example, a backup administrator is responsible for taking backups of important data. Therefore, he is only authorized to access this data for backing it up. However, sometimes users with different roles need to access the same resources. This situation can also be handled using the RBAC model.

Answer option C is incorrect. The Discretionary access control (DAC) model has an access policy determined by the owner of an object. The owner decides who is allowed to access the object and what privileges they have.

Answer option D is incorrect. An access control list (ACL) model has a list of permissions attached to an object. The list specifies who or what is allowed to access the object and what operations are allowed to be performed on the object.

Chapter 2 - First Responder Procedure, CSIRT and Computer Forensic Lab

Overview

First responder procedures are the steps and instructions, which are to be followed strictly when incidents occur. To follow the correct procedures is very important in terms of thorough and accurate investigation, and in terms of evidential requirements. The generic processes of First Responder Procedures are as follows:

- Protect the system and resources.

- Contain the intrusion.

- Preserve the evidence (logs, files, etc) in a legally acceptable way.

- Notify Managment, Incidence Response, etc.

Key Points

Forensic Process and Collecting Evidences

- Forensic process includes the methodology of the steps taken during any forensic investigation. The forensics process includes and is not limited to preparation, collection, examination, analysis, and reporting. Each phase feeds the next phase in the process. The first responder is an integral part of the collection phase.

- Volatile evidences are the data stored in temporary storage media (Random Access Memory(RAM), Cache Memory, Onboard memory of different peripherals like Graphics and video card, etc.) because data stored in it depends on the electricity for their existence, as soon as the system is powered off, stored data will be permanently vanished. It is, therefore, very important to collect such data first for investigation.

- Disk imaging is the technique that is used to preserve the original evidence as it was seized. Disk imaging is different from back up of a disk in a way that while creating a backup, only active files of a system are copied, whereas during disk imaging exact replica of original disk is formed.

- Retaining the Date and Time of creation, and modification of Data is a vital factor to be kept in mind in criminal issues. Timestamp in a file is a very important evidence, since the timestamp is according to the system clock, which in turn depends on the time zone. It can be investigated that which time zone is configured on the system. It may be possible that criminal deliberately changes the time zone so that the data does not co-relate with the real time.

Pop Quiz

Q1: Which algorithm produces a digital signature which is used to authenticate the bit-stream images?

Ans: MD5

Q2: Which of the following types of write blocker device uses one interface for one side and a different one for the other?

Ans: Taligate

- Collection of Evidence is the sole reason behind the Forensic Investigation; therefore, Evidence plays a vital role in Computer Forensic Investigation. The Digital Evidence should be properly studied, preserved and presented. These Evidences are presented in court during legal process and questioning. Collection of Evidence is done in several steps, first of which is Identification of Evidence followed by the Recovery of Evidence. This is accomplished viewing log files, recovering data using different forensic tools. One more important point, which should be kept in mind during Investigation is the security of Data. Digital Evidence and Data must be secured throughout the investigation.

- Electronic evidence is any data stored or transmitted with electronic devices. As a first responder, it is imperative to understand the types of information devices can hold.

- The collection phase of forensics is the phase where first responders are handling incidents. As mentioned before, the collection phase is critical to any investigation. The first responder should minimize any loss of electronic evidence.

Pop Quiz

Q1: Which system apply forensically desired functions such as hashing options to the data burned to disk?

Ans: FAR System

Q2: Which of the following groups provides tools and creates procedures for testing and validating computer forensic software?

Ans: NIST

Structure and Overview of CSIRT

- Computer Security Incident Response Team (CSIRT) is a name given to expert groups that handle computer security incidents. Most groups append the abbreviation CSIRT or CERT to their designations where the latter stands for Computer Emergency Response Team. For some teams the spelling of CERT refers to Computer Emergency Readiness Team while handling the same tasks. In English-speaking parts of the world, some teams took on the more specific name of CSIRT to point out the task of handling security incidents instead of other tech support work. The history of CSIRTs is linked to the existence of computer worms. Whenever a new technology arrives, its misuse is not long in following - the first worm in the IBM VNET was covered up. Shortly later a worm hit the Internet on the 3 November 1988, when the so-called Morris Worm paralyzed a good percentage of it. This led to the formation of the first Computer Emergency Response Team at Carnegie Mellon University under U.S. Government contract.

- Computer security incident is a variable term for every organization. It is required to define standard of a computer security incident for their Website. It may be as follows:

  Any real or suspected adverse event in relation to the security of computer systems or computer networks.

- Computer security incident activity can be described as a network or host activity that can be used to threaten the security of computer systems.

- Computer security incident should include various activities related to the computers; some of them are as follows:

  o Attempts to gain unauthorized access to a system or its data.

  o Unwanted disruption or denial of service.

  o Unauthorized use of a system for the processing or storage of data.

  o Changes to system hardware, software characteristics without the knowledge of the owner.

- Computer security incident is important because the information security infrastructure cannot guarantee that the intrusions and other hacking attacks will not happen. When computer security incidents occur, it is vital for an organization to have an effective way to proceed.

- Limit of the damage and the cost of recovery directly depend on the pace with which an organization can recognize, analyze, and respond to an incident. A CSIRT team is able to conduct a fast response to contain a computer security incident and recover from it. It may also have familiarity with the systems that are compromised and therefore they are able to coordinate the recovery and propose mitigation and response strategies more comfortably.

- An incident response team consists team members with various job objectives; these representatives perform a variety of roles.

- Incident handling is a process that includes three important functions, which are: incident reporting, incident analysis, and incident response.

- Incident reporting function permits a CSIRT to act as a central point for reporting local problems. This allows all incident reports and activities to be accumulated and analyzed at one location; then from here information can be reviewed and correlated across the organization. This information can then be utilized in determining the trends and patterns of malicious intruder activity and preventative strategies and methodology for the whole organization.

- Incident analysis involves in-depth investigation of the incident report or incident activity to establish the priority and threat of the incident. Incident analys is also used in researching possible response and mitigation strategies.

- Incident response function can take many forms. A CSIRT sends out their recommendations and solutions for recovery and prevention to the systems and network administrators at the site of incident, who then perform the appropriate response steps specified by CSIRT. A CSIRT may also carry out these steps themselves on the affected systems. The response may also involve sharing information and lessons learned with other response teams and other appropriate organizations and sites.

Pop Quiz

Q1: Which group is responsible for the computer security incident within an organization?

Ans: CSIRT

Q2: What is the famous name of the CSIRT?

Ans: CERT

Parameters and Requirements of Forensic Lab

- Standard Operating Procedure (SOP) describes the best practice approach to executing tasks related to the production and maintenance of hardware and software, as well as incident and change management. There are a number of solutions available to automate the execution of SOPs for large enterprises, as it pertains to information technology, such as Creekpath, iConclude, and Stratavia

- Federal Rules of Civil Procedure (FRCP) have impacted the manner in which digital information is managed in civil prosecution. The FRCP generalized the role of digital information in a legal environment.The rules have formally identified the role of electronically stored information (ESI) and how it will be handled and presented in a judicial setting.

- Overall layout of a forensic laboratory is divided into may parts, but attention should be given to at least four functional areas, which are: administrative area, examination space, network facilities, and evidence storage.

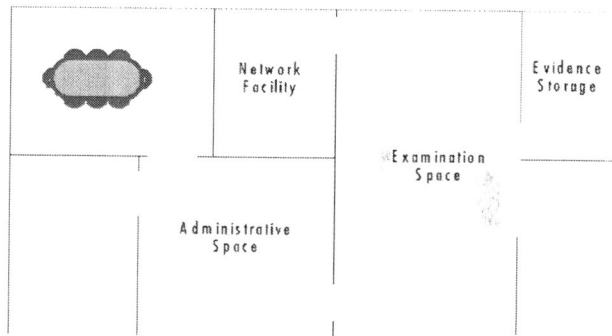

- Fire protected safe in a locked room with accurate hand-written access logs may prove sufficient security for a small environment. Other evidence storage environments implement a shelf-and-cage methodology with a single portal of entry that is key-locked and monitored for access.

- Write blockers are devices that allow acquisition of information on a drive without creating the possibility of accidentally damaging the drive contents. They do this by allowing read commands to pass but by blocking write commands.

- There are two ways to build a write-blocker: the blocker can allow all commands to pass from the computer to the drive except for those that are on a particular list. Alternatively, the blocker can specifically block the write commands and let everything else through. Write blockers may also include drive protection which will limit the speed of a drive attached to the blocker. Drives that run at a higher speed work harder (the head moves back and forth more often due to read errors). This added protection could allow drives that can not be read at high speeds (UDMA modes) to be read at the slower modes (PIO).

- There are two types of write blockers, Native and Tailgate. A Native device uses the same interface on for both in and out, for example an IDE to IDE write block. A Tailgate device uses one interface for one side and a different one for the other side, for example a Firewire to SATA write block.

Pop Quiz

Q1: What is the desired temperature operating range for a typical Data center?

Ans: 68-70 F

Q2: IWhich systems apply forensically desired functions such as hashing options to the data burned to disk?

Ans: FAR System

Key Terms

CSIRT	Computer Security Incident Response Team
SOP	Standard Operating Procedure
IDS	Intrusion Detection System
HIDS	Host-based Intrusion Detection System

Test Your Knowledge

Q1.   TCP FIN scanning is a type of stealth scanning through which the attacker sends a FIN packet to the target port. If the port is closed, the victim assumes that this packet was sent mistakenly by the attacker and sends the RST packet to the attacker. If the port is open, the FIN packet will be ignored and the port will drop the packet. Which of the following operating systems can be easily identified with the help of TCP FIN scanning?

   A.   Windows
   B.   Red Hat
   C.   Solaris
   D.   Knoppix

Q2.   Which of the following types of firewall ensures that the packets are part of the established session?

   A.   Circuit-level firewall

   B.   Application-level firewall

   C.   Stateful inspection firewall

   D.   Switch-level firewall

Q3.   Which of the following is the correct order of digital investigations Standard Operating Procedure (SOP)?

   A.   Request for service, initial analysis, data collection, data analysis, data reporting

   B.   Initial analysis, request for service, data collection, data analysis, data reporting

   C.   Request for service, initial analysis, data collection, data reporting, data analysis

   D.   Initial analysis, request for service, data collection, data reporting, data analysis

Q4.   Which of the following types of firewall functions at the Session layer of OSI model?

   A.   Packet filtering firewall
   B.   Circuit-level firewall

    C.   Application-level firewall

    D.   Switch-level firewall

Q5. You work as a Network Administrator for NetTech Inc. The company's network is connected to the Internet. For security, you want to restrict unauthorized access to the network with minimum administrative effort. You want to implement a hardware-based solution. What will you do to accomplish this?

    A.   Implement firewall on the network.

    B.   Implement a proxy server on the network.

    C.   Connect a brouter to the network.

    D.   Connect a router to the network.

Answer Explanation

A1.   Answer option A is correct.

Windows operating systems send only RST packets irrespective of whether the target port is open or closed. Hence, Windows can be easily identified with the help of TCP FIN scanning.

Answer options B, C, and D are incorrect. If the port is closed, these operating systems send the RST packets to the attacker, and, if the port is open, they simply ignore the FIN packet.

A2.   Answer option C is correct.

The stateful inspection firewall combines the circuit level and the application level firewall techniques. It assures the session or connection between the two parties is valid. It also inspects packets from the session to assure that the packets are part of the established session and not malicious.

Answer option A is incorrect. The circuit-level firewall regulates traffic based on whether or not a trusted connection has been established.

Answer option B is incorrect. The application level firewall inspects the contents of packets, rather than the source/destination or connection between the two devices.

Answer option D is incorrect. There is no firewall type such as switch-level firewall.

A3.   Answer option C is correct.

A standard operating procedure is a set of instructions having the force of a directive, covering those features of operations that lend themselves to a definite or standardized procedure without loss of effectiveness. Standard Operating Policies and Procedures can be effective catalysts to drive performance improvement and improve organizational results. Every good quality system is based on its standard operating procedures (SOPs). Steps of standard operating procedures are as follows:

   1. Request for service

2. Initial analysis

3. Data collection

4. Data analysis

5. Data reporting

Answer options A, B, and D are incorrect. All these are not the correct order of digital investigations Standard Operating Procedure (SOP).

Standard Operating Procedure (SOP) describes a best practice approach to executing tasks related to the production and maintenance of hardware and software, as well as incident and change management. There are a number of solutions available to automate the execution of SOPs for large enterprises, as it pertains to information technology, such as Creekpath, iConclude and Stratavia.

A4. Answer option B is correct.

Circuit-level firewall operates at the Session layer of the OSI model. This type of firewall regulates traffic based on whether or not a trusted connection has been established.

Answer option A is incorrect. Packet filtering firewall operates at the network layer of the OSI model.

Answer option C is incorrect. Application-level firewall operates at the application layer of the OSI model.

Answer option D is incorrect. There is no firewall type such as Switch-level firewall.

A5. Answer option A is correct.

Firewall is available both as software and hardware. You can implement hardware-based firewall for security with minimum administrative effort.

Firewall is used to protect an internal network or intranet against unauthorized access from the Internet or other networks. It restricts inbound and outbound access and can analyze all traffic between an internal network and the Internet. Users can configure a firewall to pass or block packets from specific IP addresses and ports.

Answer option B is incorrect. A firewall is also in-built within a proxy server. Although implementing a proxy server on the network will implement the firewall automatically, it will be a software-based solution.

Answer option C is incorrect. A brouter is a combination of a bridge and a router. It is used to connect dissimilar network segments, and it routes only a specific transport protocol such as TCP/IP. A brouter also works as a bridge for all types of packets, passing them on as long as they are not local to the LAN segment from which they have originated.

Answer option D is incorrect. Router is a device that routes data packets between computers in different networks. It is used to connect multiple networks, and it determines the path to be taken by each data packet to its destination computer. Router maintains a routing table of the available routes and their conditions. By using this information, along with distance and cost algorithms, the router determines the best path to be taken by the data packets to the destination computer. A router can connect dissimilar networks, such as Ethernet, FDDI, and Token Ring, and route data packets among them. Routers operate at the network layer (layer 3) of the Open Systems Interconnection (OSI) model.

Chapter 3 - Understanding File System, Hard Disk, and Digital media devices, Windows, Linux and Macintosh Boot

Overview

A file system is a method for storing and organizing computer files and the data they contain to make it easy to find and access them. File systems may use a data storage device such as a hard disk or CD-ROM and involve maintaining the physical location of the files, they might provide access to data on a file server by acting as clients for a network protocol (e.g., NFS, SMB, or 9P clients), or they may be virtual and exist only as an access method for virtual data (e.g., procfs). It is distinguished from a directory service and registry. More formally, a file system is a special-purpose database for the storage, organization, manipulation, and retrieval of data. ost file systems make use of an underlying data storage device that offers access to an array of fixed-size blocks, sometimes called sectors, generally a power of 2 in size (512 bytes or 1, 2, or 4 Kb are most common). The file system software is responsible for organizing these sectors into files and directories, and keeping track of which sectors belong to which file and which are not being used. Most file systems address data in fixed-sized units called "clusters" or "blocks" which contain a certain number of disk sectors (usually 1-64). This is the smallest amount of disk space that can be allocated to hold a file. However, file systems need not make use of a storage device at all. A file system can be used to organize and represent access to any data, whether it be stored or dynamically generated.

Key Points

Different Hard Disk Interfaces and Capacity Calculation

- RAID is described as a redundant array of inexpensive disks. It is a technology that allows computer users to achieve high levels of storage reliability from low-cost and less reliable PC-class disk-drive components, via the technique of arranging the devices into arrays for redundancy. RAID is now used as an umbrella term for computer data storage schemes that can divide and replicate data among multiple hard disk drives.

- The different schemes/architectures are named by the word RAID followed by a number, as in RAID 0, RAID 1, etc. Various designs of RAID involve two key design goals: increased data reliability or increased input/output performance. When multiple physical disks are set up to use RAID technology, they are said to be in a RAID array. This array distributes data across multiple disks, but the array is seen by the computer user and operating system as one single disk. RAID can be set up to serve several different purposes.

- The Optical Storage Technology Association (OSTA) is an international trade association, which promotes the use of recordable optical technologies and products, and most notably it is responsible for the creation and maintenance of the UDF specification. Representing more than 85 percent of worldwide writable optical product shipment's manufacturers and resellers, it was incorporated in 1992.

- IDE (Integrated Drive Electronics) or ATA (Advanced Technology Attachment) is a standard interfacing technology for the connection of storage devices like hard disk, and solid state devices. This standard is maintained by American National Standard Institute (ANSI). IDE is named so because the disk controller is integrated in the mother board of the computer. ATA/ATAPI (ATA Packet Interface) is an evolution of the AT Attachment Interface.

- Parallel ATA standard is the result of technical development in the field of AT Attachment interface. It allows cable lengths of up to 46 cm, therefore normally used as an internal computer storage interface.

- The Serial ATA (SATA), computer bus is a storage-interface for connecting host bus adapters to mass storage devices such as hard disk drives and optical drives. Serial ATA was designed to replace the older ATA (AT Attachment) standard (Parallel ATA). It uses the same low level commands, but serial ATA host-adapters and devices communicate via a high-speed serial cable over two pairs of conductors. SATA provides numerous advantages over Parallel ATA interface.Windows Server 2008 has the following new server roles: RODC, ADLDS, ADRMS, and ADFS.

Pop Quiz

Q1: Which units is the largest unit used to describe the capacity of disks?

Ans: Yottabyte (Yb)

Q2: Which of the following is the most secure file system offered by Microsoft Windows?

Ans: NTFS

- Bad sectors, in a hard disk, are formed due to manufacturing defects or accidental damage. These sectors are not able to store data further. Under different OS environment, various Tools and Programs are available to scan and mark the bad sectors in a hard disk.

- Hard disk interface is a standard technology used to connect the hard disk to the computer. This interface serves as a communication channel, to provide bi-directional data flow.

- Calculation of the hard disk capacity includes various constructional parameters and elements of the disk, including the number of tracks, sectors etc., on which data can be written.

- SATA is faster, more efficient in data transfer, and reduces cable-bulk.

Various File Systems

- NTFS is a high-performance file system proprietary to Microsoft. NTFS supports file-level security, compression, and auditing. It also supports large volumes and powerful storage solution such as RAID. The latest feature of NTFS is its ability to encrypt files and folders to protect sensitive data.

- NTFS supports compression on volumes, folders, and files. Files that are compressed on an NTFS volume can be read and written by any Windows-based application without first being decompressed by another program. Decompression takes place automatically at the time the file is being read. The file gets compressed again when it is closed or saved.

- Cluster remapping is a recovery technique employed by the NTFS file system. Whenever a Windows operating system employing an NTFS file system generates a bad-sector error, NTFS dynamically replaces the disk cluster containing the corrupt sector and allocates a new disk cluster to the corresponding data. If the error occurs during a read operation, NTFS returns a read error to the calling program and the corresponding data is lost, unless there was some fault tolerance method (e.g., RAID) in place. However, if the error occurs during a write operation, NTFS writes the data to a new disk cluster. Hence, no data is lost. NTFS records the address of the cluster containing the bad sector in its bad sector file. Hence, the bad sector is not reused.

- By default, when a parent folder is assigned NTFS permissions, the permissions also propagate or apply to the subfolders and files that are either already within the parent folder or have been newly created within the parent folder. The permissions applied on the subfolders in this way are called inherited permissions. When an administrator assigns NTFS permissions to a folder, all existing subfolders and files or newly created folders and files with the parent folder inherit the permissions of the parent folder. A user can prevent automatic propagation of NTFS permissions to subfolders and files within the parent folder. The directory or folder level on which the user decides to prevent the default NTFS permission inheritance becomes the new parent folder for NTFS permission inheritance.

- VFAT (Virtual File Allocation Table) is a 32-bit file system that Windows 95 and NT use to manage information stored on disks. It is an extension of the FAT file system, VFAT supports long filenames (256 characters) and 32-bit protected mode access while retaining compatibility with FAT volumes.

- File Allocation Table or FAT is a computer file system architecture now widely used on most computer systems and most memory cards, such as those used with digital cameras. It was developed by Bill Gates and Marc McDonald during 1976-1977. It is the primary file system for various operating systems including DR-DOS, FreeDOS, MS-DOS, OS/2 (v1.1) and Microsoft Windows. For floppy disks, it has been standardized as ECMA-107 and ISO/IEC 9293. Those standards include only FAT12 and FAT16 without long filename support; long filenames with FAT is partially patented. The FAT file system is relatively straightforward technically and is supported by virtually all existing operating systems for personal computers. This makes it a useful format for solid-state memory cards and a convenient way to share data between operating systems.

- In order to overcome the volume size limit of FAT16, while still allowing DOS real mode code to handle the format without unnecessarily reducing the available conventional memory, Microsoft implemented a newer generation of FAT, known as FAT32, with cluster values held in a 32-bit field, of which 28 bits are used to hold the cluster number, for a maximum of approximately 268 million (228) clusters. This allows for drive sizes of up to 8 terabytes with 32KB clusters, but the boot sector uses a 32-bit field for the sector count, limiting volume size to 2 TB on a hard disk with 512 byte sectors. FAT32 was introduced with Windows 95 OSR2, although reformatting was needed to use it, and DriveSpace 3 (the version that came with Windows 95 OSR2 and Windows 98) never supported it. Windows 98 introduced a utility to convert existing hard disks from FAT16 to FAT32 without loss of data.

- ISO 9660, also referred to as CDFS (Compact Disc File System) by some hardware and software providers, is a file system standard published by the International Organization for Standardization (ISO) for optical disc media. It aims at supporting different computer operating systems such as Windows, classic Mac OS, and Unix-like systems, so that data may be exchanged. ISO 9660 traces its roots to the High Sierra file system. High Sierra arranged file information in a dense, sequential layout to minimize non-sequential access by using a hierarchical (eight levels of directories deep) tree file system arrangement, similar to UNIX and FAT. To facilitate cross platform compatibility, it defined a minimal set of common file attributes (directory or ordinary file and time of recording) and name attributes (name, extension, and version), and used a separate system use area where future optional extensions for each file may be specified.

- exFAT (Extended File Allocation Table) is a proprietary file system suited especially for flash drives, introduced by Microsoft for embedded devices in Windows Embedded CE 6.0 and in their desktop operating system. exFAT can be used where the NTFS file system is not a feasible solution, due to data structure overhead, or where the file size or directory restrictions of the FAT file system are unacceptable. Windows XP users can add support for exFAT by installing an update from Microsoft. An experimental Linux kernel module that supports the reading of exFAT files is currently under development.

- The NTFS file system supports a feature called hot fixing. In this process, the operating system detects a bad sector on the disk and automatically relocates the data stored on that sector to a new good sector, and then marks the bad sector so that the system does not use it again. This process happens in the background without the awareness or interference of the user or applications.

- The Master File Table (MFT) is the table where information of each and every files and directory on an NTFS file system is stored. The MFT contains various parameters about different files. MFT acts as the "starting point" of an NTFS file system. MFT is similar to the file allocation table in a FAT file system. When a file is created on the NTFS file system, MFT creates a record for it. Each record is equal to the cluster size of the volume, but with a minimum of 1,024 bytes and a maximum of 4,096 byte. The system uses these MFT files to store information about the files or directory. This information is in the form of attributes and features.

- The Encrypting File System (EFS) is a file system driver that provides file system-level encryption in Microsoft Windows operating systems. It also exists in IBM AIX operating system. The technology enables files to be transparently encrypted on NTFS file systems to protect confidential data from attackers with physical access to the computer. User authentication and access control lists can protect files from unauthorized access while the operating system is running, but are easily circumvented if an attacker gains physical access to the computer. One solution is to store the files encrypted on the disks of the computer. EFS does this using public key cryptography, and aims to ensure that decrypting the files is extremely difficult without the correct key. However, EFS is in practice susceptible to brute-force attacks against the user account passwords. In other words, encryption of files is only as strong as the password to unlock the decryption key.

- Journaled File System (JFS) is a 64-bit journaling file system created by IBM. It is available as free software under the terms of the GNU General Public License (GPL). In the Linux operating system, JFS is supported with the kernel module and the complementary user space utilities packaged under the name JFSutils. Most Linux distributions provide support for JFS, unless it is specifically removed due to space restrictions or other concerns. JFS is fast and reliable, with consistently good performance under different kinds of load, contrary to other file systems that seem to perform better under particular usage patterns, for instance with small or large files. Another characteristic often mentioned is that it is light and efficient with available system resources, and even heavy disk activity is realized with low CPU usage.

- The Universal Disk Format (UDF) is a format specification of a file system for storing files on optical media. It is an implementation of the ISO/IEC 13346 standard (also known as ECMA-167). It is considered to be a replacement for ISO 9660, and is widely used for (re)writable optical media.

- UDF is developed and maintained by the Optical Storage Technology Association (OSTA). This format can be used on any type of disk that allows random read/write access, such as hard disks, DVD+RW and DVD-RAM media. Similarly to other common file system formats, such as FAT, directory entries point directly to the block numbers of their file contents. In writing to such a disk in this format, any physical block on the disk may be chosen for allocation of new or updated files. Since this is the basic format, practically any OS or File System Driver claiming support for UDF should be able to read this format.

- In computing, ZFS is a combined file system and logical volume manager designed by Sun Microsystems. The features of ZFS include support for high storage capacities, integration of the concepts of file system and volume management, snapshots and copy-on-write clones, continuous integrity checking and automatic repair, RAID-Z and native NFSv4 ACLs. ZFS is implemented as open-source software, licensed under the Common Development and Distribution License (CDDL). The ZFS name is a trade mark of Sun.

- Hierarchical File System (HFS), is a file system developed by Apple Inc. for use in computer systems running Mac OS. Originally designed for use on floppy and hard disks, it can also be found on read-only media such as CD-ROMs. HFS is also referred to as Mac OS Standard, where its successor, HFS Plus, is also called Mac OS Extended. With the introduction of OS X 10.6, Apple has dropped support to format or write HFS disks and images, which are only supported as read-only volumes. ADLDS is used for providing services to directory-aware applications. It is very useful to install it where there is no need for the overhead of a complete forest or domain structure.

- FAT16 file system was developed for disks larger than 16MB. It uses 16-bit allocation table entries.

- FAT16 file system supports all Microsoft operating systems. It also supports OS/2 and Linux.

- NTFS file system supports a feature called hot fixing. In this process, the operating system detects a bad sector on the disk and automatically relocates the data stored on that sector to a new good sector, and then marks the bad sector so that the system won't use it again.

- The Master File Table (MFT) is a table where information of each and every file and directory on an NTFS file system is stored.

- EFS uses public key cryptography and digital certificates to encrypt the data stored on a disk on a file-by-file basis.

- The third Extended File System or ext3 of Linux is a journaled file system.

Boot Processes of different OS

- Power On Self Test (POST) is a small program stored in a Read Only Memory (ROM) Basic Input Output System (BIOS) of a computer system starting at address hf000. This program tests the basic motherboard functions such as power supply, memory, buses, interfaces, etc. and reports any error with audio beep codes. It also sends diagnostic code to internal port h80 if an error occurs.

- Diagnostic codes are different error codes send by most modern computers to internal port h80 if an error occurs. These diagnostic codes are read by the diagnostic cards, which can plug into the ISA/PCI/AGP slots on motherboard and provide more descriptive and comprehensive error reports.

100 to 199	System boards
200 to 299	Memory
300 to 399	Keyboard

400 to 499	Monochrome display
500 to 599	Color/graphics display
600 to 699	Floppy-disk drive or adapter
700 to 799	Math coprocessor
900 to 999	Parallel printer port
1000 to 1099	Alternate printer adapter
1100 to 1299	Asynchronous communication device, adapter, or port
1300 to 1399	Game port
1400 to 1499	Color/graphics printer
1500 to 1599	Synchronous communication device, adapter, or port
1700 to 1799	Hard drive and/or adapter
1800 to 1899	Expansion unit (XT)
2000 to 2199	Bisynchronous communication adapter
2400 to 2599	EGA system-board video (MCA)
3000 to 3199	LAN adapter
4800 to 4999	Internal modem
7300 to 7399	3.5-inch disk drive
8900 to 8999	MIDI adapter
11200 to 11299	SCSI adapter
21000 to 21099	SCSI fixed disk
21500 to 21599	SCSI CD-ROM system

- The Master Boot Sector (MBR) is a 512 bytes long boot sector that is the first sector of a default boot drive. It is also known as Volume Boot Sector, if the boot drive is un-partitioned. When the MBR is found, the program is tested and loaded to ensure that the last two bytes are h55AA. Actual program is only 444 bytes long. Structure of the MBR is as follows:

Structure of a Master Boot Record

Address			Description	Size in bytes
Hex	Oct	Dec		
0000	0000	0	Code Area	440 (max. 446)
01B8	0670	440	Optional Disk signature	4
01BC	0674	444	Usually Nulls; 0x0000	2
01BE	0676	446	**Table of primary partitions** (Four 16-byte entries, IBM Partition Table scheme)	64
01FE	0776	510	55h — MBR signature; 0xAA55[1]	2
01FF	0777	511	AAh —	
MBR, total size: 446 + 64 + 2 =				**512**

- A Bootloader is a program that runs when a Computer starts. The bootloader is responsible for loading an operating system for the Computer. It may perform number of actions, but its main function is to place the computer in a state from where the Operating system can start in. It usually contains different methods to boot the OS Kernel and also contains the command for debugging. It starts the sequence of loading small programs into RAM that finally results in loading of Operating System.

- Loading Windows XP on a computer includes various system files. Every file has a specific job and objective and it is very necessary that these files execute in a pre-defined order. The Sequence of loading system files in Windows XP is: NTLDR, BOOT.ini, NTDETECT.com, HAL.dll, NTOSKRNL.exe.

- The Extensible Firmware Interface (EFI) is a specification that defines a software interface between an operating system and platform firmware. EFI is a much larger, more complex, OS-like: for replacement of the older BIOS firmware interface present in all IBM PC-compatible personal computers. The EFI specification was originally developed by Intel, and is now managed by the Unified EFI Forum.

- Snag keys are the single keys, which when pressed allow the system to boot from specific devices. This is the optional startup functions based on user input provided by Extensible Firmware Interface (EFI) in Mac OS X.

- The Berkeley Software Distribution (BSD) portion of the kernel provides the primary system program interface, the Unix process model atop Mach tasks, basic security policies, user and group ids, permissions, the network stack, the virtual file system code (including a file system independent journaling layer), Network File System (NFS), cryptographic framework, UNIX System V inter-process communication (IPC), Audit subsystem, Mandatory Access Control and some of the locking primitives. The BSD code present in XNU came from the FreeBSD kernel. Although much of it has been significantly modified, code sharing still occurs between Apple and the FreeBSD Project.

- Mach is the core of the XNU kernel. It was originally conceived as a simple microkernel. As such, it is able to run the core of an operating system as separated processes, which allows a great flexibility, but this often reduces performance because of time consuming kernel/user mode context switches and overhead stemming from mapping or copying messages between the address spaces of the microkernel and that of the service daemons. With Mac OS X, the designers have attempted to streamline certain tasks and thus BSD functionalities were built into the core with Mach.

- Mach provides kernel threads, processes, pre-emptive multitasking, message-passing, protected memory, virtual memory management, very soft real-time support, kernel debugging support, and console I/O. The Mach component also allows the OS to host binaries for multiple distinct CPU architectures within a single file due to its use of the Mach-O binary format.

- I/O Toolkit is the device driver framework, written in a subset of C++. Using its object-oriented design, features common to any class of driver are provided within the framework itself, helping device drivers be written more quickly and using less code. The I/O Toolkit is multi-threaded, Symmetric multiprocessing (SMP)-safe, and allows for hot pluggable devices and automatic, dynamic device configuration. Many drivers can be written to run from user-space, which further enhances the stability of the system; if a user-space driver crashes, it will not crash the kernel. However, if a kernel-space driver crashes it will crash the kernel. Examples of kernel-space drivers include Parallels, EyeTV and the Apple USB driver.

- The LIBKERN is the collection and container of the classes, which offers powerful services to drivers to configure its runtime environment. The LIBKERN classes offer numerous advantages, such as object introspection, and encapsulation. The LIBKERN container and collection classes closely resemble to the Core Foundation classes in name and behavior. This provides the system to automatically translate between LIBKERN and Core Foundation classes of the same type.

- XNU is the computer operating system kernel that Apple Inc. acquired and developed for use in the Mac OS X operating system and released as free and open source software as part of the Darwin operating system. Originally developed by NeXT for the NEXTSTEP operating system, XNU was a hybrid kernel combining version 2.5 of the Mach kernel developed at Carnegie Mellon University with components from 4.3BSD and an object-oriented API for writing drivers called Driver Kit. After Apple acquired NeXT, the Mach component was upgraded to 3.0, the BSD components were upgraded with code from the FreeBSD project and the Driver Kit was replaced with a C++ API for writing drivers called I/O Kit.

- Loading Windows XP on a computer includes various system files. Every file has a specific job and objective and it is very necessary that these files execute in a pre-defined order.

- XNU is the computer operating system kernel that Apple Inc. acquired and developed for use in the Mac OS X operating system and released as free and open source software as part of the Darwin operating system. XNU comprises various modules.

Pop Quiz

Q1: What is the name of the group of blocks which contains information used by the operating system in Linux system?

Ans: superblock

Q2: Which parts of hard disk in Mac OS X File system stores information related to the files?

Ans: Resource fork

- There are some pre-defined steps for searching data on Windows system, which is necessary for proper and efficient investigation and analysis of the data collected.

- POST tests the basic motherboard functions and reports any errors with audio beep codes. Different beep codes refer to different types of errors.

- Diagnostic codes are different error codes sent by most modern computers to internal port h80 if an error occurs. These diagnostic codes are read by the diagnostic cards, which can plug into the ISA/PCI/AGP slots on motherboard and provide more descriptive and comprehensive error reports.

- The BIOS scans memory for ROM in the range of hC800 to hDF80, which may contain any additional codes that are required to be executed for other adapter cards such as sound cards, RAID arrays, etc.

- The Master Boot Sector (MBR) is a 512 bytes long boot sector that is the first sector of a default boot drive. It is also known as Volume Boot Sector, if the boot drive is un-partitioned. When the MBR is found, the program is tested and loaded to ensure that the last two bytes are h55AA. Actual program is only 444 bytes long.

- Linux Loader (LILO) is the default boot loader (boot manager) for most of the Linux systems. It is used to boot a computer into Linux. LILO provides many tools for troubleshooting booting issues. It also allows a dual boot of the Linux operating system with any other operating system.

- "/boot/grub/menu.lst" is the GRUB configuration file of Debian Linux operating system.

- Snag keys are the single keys, which when pressed allow the system to boot from specific devices. This are optional startup functions based on user input provided by Extensible Firmware Interface (EFI) in Mac OS X.

- ADFS requires either the Windows Server 2008 Enterprise edition or the Datacenter edition.

Key Terms

POST	Power On Self Test
MBR	Master Boot Sector
exFAT	Extended File Allocation Table
MFT	Master File Table
JFS	Journaled File System
EFS	Encrypting File System
OSTA	Optical Storage Technology Association

EFI   Extensible Firmware Interface

BSD   Berkeley Software Distribution

Test Your Knowledge

Q1. Which of the following is used to detect the bad sectors in a hard disk under Linux environment?

A.   CHKDSK

B.   CheckDisk

C.   Badblocks

D.   ScanDisk

Q2. Which of the following standard technologies is not used to interface hard disk with the computer?

A.   PS/2

B.   IDE/ATA

C.   USB

D.   SCSI

Q3. Which of the following parameters is NOT used for calculating the capacity of the hard disk?

A.   Bytes per sector

B.   Number of heads

C.   Number of platters

D.   Total number of sectors

Q4. Which of the following statements is NOT true about FAT16 file system?

Each correct answer represents a complete solution. Choose all that apply.

A.   FAT16 file system works well with large disks because the cluster size increases as the disk partition size increases.

B.   FAT16 file system supports file-level compression.

C.   FAT16 file system supports Linux operating system.

D.   FAT16 does not support file-level security.

Q5. Which of the following file systems supports the hot fixing feature?

A.   FAT32

B.   FAT16

C.   NTFS

D.   exFAT

Answer Explanation

A1.   Answer option C is correct.

Badblocks is a tool used in Linux system. This tool detects the damaged sectors of the hard disk and marks them as Bad.

Answer options A, B, and D are incorrect. CheckDisk and ScanDisk are programs used in Windows system to detect damaged sectors of the hard disk. CHKDSK is the notation of CheckDisk in DOS 8.3.

A2.   Answer option A is correct.

The PS/2 (Personal System/2) connector is used to connect Mouse and Keyboard to the computer.

Answer options B, C, and D are incorrect.

IDE/ATA (Integrated Drive Electronics), USB (Universal Serial Bus), and SCSI (Small Computer System Interface) are different Hard disk interfacing technologies. These interfaces are used for connecting the hard disk to the computer.

A3.   Answer option C is correct.

Number of platters does not play any role in the calculation of disk capacity. Data is stored on the surface of platter in the form of tracks and sectors.

Answer options A, B, and D are incorrect. Bytes per sector, number of heads and the total number of sectors are used to calculate the capacity of hard disk.

Following formula is used for calculating the hard disk capacity:

Capacity of hard disk = Bytes per sector x number of cylinders x number of heads x sectors

A4.   Answer options A and B are correct.

FAT16 file system was developed for disks larger than 16MB. It uses 16-bit allocation table entries. FAT16 file system supports all Microsoft operating systems. It also supports OS/2 and Linux.

Answer options C and are incorrect. All these statements are true about FAT16 file system.

A5.   Answer option C is correct.

The NTFS file system supports a feature called hot fixing. In this process, the operating system detects a bad sector on the disk and automatically relocates the data stored on that sector to a new good sector, and then marks the bad sector so that the system does not use it again. This process happens in the background without the awareness or interference of the user or applications.

Answer option A is incorrect. The FAT32 file system does not support hot fixing. The FAT32 file system is an enhancement of the FAT file system. It is more advanced and reliable than all the earlier versions of the FAT file system. It manages storage space on large hard disks more efficiently than the FAT16 file system. It uses a smaller cluster size than the FAT16 file system on the hard disk, thereby reducing the amount of space on the hard disk when users save small files. The FAT32 file system supports hard disk drives larger than 2GB and up to 2TB.

Answer option B is incorrect. The FAT16 file system does not support hot fixing.

Answer option D is incorrect. The exFAT file system does not support hot fixing. exFAT (Extended File Allocation Table) is a proprietary file system suited especially for flash drives, introduced by Microsoft for embedded devices in Windows Embedded CE 6.0 and in their desktop operating system. exFAT can be used where the NTFS file system is not a feasible solution, due to data structure overhead, or where the file size or directory restrictions of the FAT file system are unacceptable. Windows XP users can add support for exFAT by installing an update from Microsoft. An experimental Linux kernel module that supports the reading of exFAT files is currently under development.

Chapter 4 - Windows and Linux Forensics, Computer Forensic tools, Forensic Investigation using encase.

Overview

Computer forensics is a branch of forensic science pertaining to legal evidence found in computers and digital storage media. Computer forensics is also known as digital forensics.

The goal of computer forensics is to explain the current state of a digital artifact. The term digital artifact can include a computer system, a storage medium (such as a hard disk or CD-ROM), an electronic document (e.g. an email message or JPEG image) or even a sequence of packets moving over a computer network. The explanation can be as straightforward as "what information is here?" and as detailed as "what is the sequence of events responsible for the present situation?"

The field of computer forensics also has sub branches within it such as firewall forensics, network forensics, database forensics and mobile device forensics.

Key Points

Windows Forensic Tools.

- WinHex is a famous hexadecimal editor tool that is used to examine files that have been collected for analysis and examination. This includes file fragments, recovered deleted files, or other data that have been corrupted or destroyed. WinHex can also examine the contents of a file retrieved from a hard disk whose application software, which opens a particular file, is not available. We can also view data captured from a network to identify passwords and other data. WinHex also provides a feature that allows cloning of a hard disk and thus making a duplicate of the data to work with. It can also provide a RAM editor feature that allows access to the physical RAM and any processes running in virtual memory. WinHex is also set to run in a write-protected mode, which open any file in a read-only mode to prevent any modification in the original data.

- Access Pass View is an application available in Windows Live side of the Helix. This application is used to reveal the database password of the password-protected MDB files, which are created by Microsoft Access or Jet Database Engine. In Access 2000/XP files, this utility cannot recover passwords that contain more than 18 characters. Access Pass View utility shows only the main database passwords. It cannot recover the user-level passwords.

- Asterisk logger is used to reveal the passwords stored behind the asterisks in standard password text box. Asterisk Logger also displays the additional information about the revealed password: The date/time that the password was revealed, the name of the application that contains the revealed password box, and the executable file of the application, etc. Asterisk Logger also provides option for saving revealed passwords in HTML and text files.

- Galleta is an application, which is used to examine the contents of the cookie files. Galleta parses the information in a Cookie file and outputs the results in a field delimited manner so that it may be imported into spreadsheet program. Galleta is built to work on various platforms and will execute on Windows (through Cygwin), Mac OS X, and Linux.

- Forensic Acquisition Utilities (FAU) is an Incident Response tool, which is used to make image of the system's memory and any device attached to the system. FAU contains a modified Windows version of the Unix utility dd that could image not only the hard drives but also the memory. With the help of Forensic Acquisition Utilities (FAU), forensic investigators can use the search tools to find text in the memory image, IP addresses, URLs and passwords.

- Forensic Server Project (FSP) is an application software, which provides a framework to perform forensic data collection from potentially compromised systems and transporting it to a server via the network interface of the system using TCP/IP. Because of this, files are not written to the potentially compromised system. FSP runs from removable media, such as a USB connected thumb drive but with little modifications to the code. It can also write data to those thumb drives. The FSP consists of several Perl scripts and third party utilities.

- The Forensic Toolkit Imager (FTK Imager) is a commercial forensic imaging software package distributed by AccessData. FTK Imager supports storage of disk images in EnCase's or SMART's file format, as well as in raw (dd) format. With Isobuster technology built in, FTK Imager Images CD's to an ISO/CUE file combination. This also includes multi and open session CDs. FTK imager acquires physical device images from FAT, NTFS, EXT 2, EXT 3, HFS, and HFS+ file systems.

- Drive Manager is an application software, which identifies the drives of the same types. Drive Manager displays the vendor information and volume label so that multiple CD/DVD drives and removable drives such as USB thumb drives can be differentiated by their manufacturers name, version and revision date. Drive Manager also shows the serial number as a unique ID for each drives.

- Vedit is a commercial text editor for Microsoft Windows and MS-DOS. Vedit was one of the pioneers in visual editing. Today, it is a powerful and feature-rich general-purpose text editor. Vedit can edit any file, including binary files and huge multi-gigabyte files. Still it is compact and extremely fast, perhaps because it is written mostly in Assembly language.

- Request for Comments (RFC) is a memorandum published by the Internet Engineering Task Force (IETF) describing methods, behaviors, research, or innovations applicable to the working of the Internet and Internet-connected systems. Through the Internet Society, engineers and computer scientists may publish discourse in the form of an RFC, either for peer review or simply to convey new concepts, information, or engineering humor. The IETF adopts some of the proposals published as RFCs as Internet standards.

- Helix is a live acquisition tool, which is used to collect volatile information. It presents a portable forensic environment, which provides access to many Windows based tools. Helix contains static binaries for Linux, Solaris and Windows using GNU utilities and Cygwin tools. These tools include Sysinternal's tools, Garners Forensic Acquisition Utilities suite, Windows Toolchest, and Windows Debugger. One of the important advantages of Helix tool is that it maintains the integrity of command line by ensuring that Windows built in command line tools do not run from the compromised system. Windows command-line tools present in Helix are as follows:

  i. cab extractor

  ii. ipconfig

  iii. kill

  iv. netstat

  v. Process explorer

- HxD is a freeware hex editor and disk editor developed by Ma l H rz for Windows. It can open files larger than 4 GB, and open and edit the raw contents of disk drives, as well as display and edit the memory used by running processes. Among other features, it can calculate various checksums and compare files. As the UPN suffix must be unique for the entire forest, add the new UPN suffix to the forest to ensure that it is available for user accounts in all the domains.

- There are some pre-defined steps for searching data on Windows system, which is necessary for proper and efficient investigation and analysis of data collected. The steps for searching for data on a Windows based system is as follows:

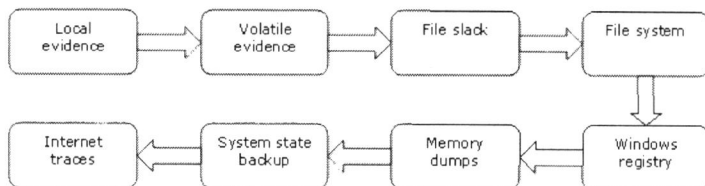

- Messen Pass is application software present in Helix Live for Windows. This software allows the recovery of passwords from numerous instant messenger programs, which are as follows:

    i.   MSN Messenger

    ii. Windows Live Messenger

    iii. Yahoo Messenger

    iv. Google Talk

    v.   AOL Instant Messenger

    vi. Trillian Astra

    vii. MySpace IM

- Messen Pass recovers both user name and passwords and save it to HTML or text files. It can only be used to recover the passwords for the current logged-on user on local computer.

- Mail PassView is a password recovery tool present in a Helix Live, which is used to reveal the passwords and other account details of various email clients, which are as follows:

    i.   Outlook Express

    ii. Windows Live Mail

    iii. IncrediMail

    iv. Eudora

    v. Mozilla Thunderbird

    vi. Yahoo! Mail

    vii. Hotmail/MSN mail

    viii. Gmail

- Mail passView displays the following fields for a particular email account: Account Name, Application, Email, Server, Server Type (POP3/IMAP/SMTP), User Name, and the Password.

- MD5 Checksum Verifier is an application, which is used as a file integrity checker. It uses MD5 algorithm to produce cryptographic hashes. MD5 Checksum Verifier creates checksums of files and verifies their integrity. This process involves two steps: Create the check file, Verify the check file.

- Chaos MD5 is a generator for Windows. It takes any file as an input and generates a MD5 checksum for that file, i.e., it generates a unique signature for each and every file. Chaos MD5 does not require installation. It works just by copying it to the hard drive or USB device to run. The MD5 checksum that is generated can be used for file identification or integrity checks.

- Mat-MD5 is a free software, which generates MD5 hashes to check the MD5 value for each file processed and compare it with other MD5 strings. It will process one or more file and add the result value to a list. MD5 values can be compared by typing it or by copying it from an external file; this will easily compare both the values.

- The Secure Hash Signature Generator is application software, which generates hash signatures that are unique to the data stored on a disk drive. These signatures are used to verify data integrity by detecting intentional or accidental tampering of drive data. The Secure Hash Signature Generator has the ability to detect up to three P-ATA, S-ATA, SCSI or ATA compatible flash devices, attached to a PC. It uses three different hash signature generating algorithms, including MD5 (128-bit signature), SHA1 (160-bit signature), and CRC32 (32-bit signature).

- A memory dump file is created when Windows crashes. This file contains valuable information, which is used to investigate why the system stopped. System requires paging file of at least 2 MB on the boot volume to produce memory dump. Memory dump files are useful in studying and analyzing memory contents during a program failure. It contains information in octal or hexadecimal form. Contents of memory dump file are as follows:

    i.   The stop message and its parameters.

    ii. A list of loaded drivers.

    iii. The processor's context (PRCB) for the processes that stopped a regular normal operation of Windows.

    iv. The kernel-mode call stack for the thread that stopped the process from execution

    v.   The process information and kernel context (ETHREAD) for the thread that stopped.

- Alternate Data Streams (ADS) is a feature of NTFS file system, which allows more than one data stream to be associated with a filename, using the filename format "filename:streamname". Alternate streams are not listed in Windows Explorer, and their size is not included in the file size. ADS provide hacker a place to hide root kits or hacker tools, which can be executed without being detected by the system administrator. Alternate Data Streams are strictly a feature of the NTFS file system. Alternate Data Streams may be used as a method of hiding executables or proprietary content.

- CHKDSK is a command-line tool used to scan and repair volumes on the hard disk for physical problems such as bad blocks. It also repairs volumes for logical structure errors such as lost clusters, cross-linked files, or directory errors.

- WinHex is a famous hexadecimal editor tool that is used to examine files that have been collected for analysis and examination. This includes file fragments, recovered deleted files, or other data that have been corrupted or destroyed.

- There are a number of locations present in the Windows host, which acts as a rich source of electronic evidences.

- RFC 3227 is a list, which specifies the order of volatility of data in a Windows based system. This list is used to collect volatile data and evidences in a particular order to avoid any error in collection of electronic evidences.

- Helix is a live acquisition tool, which is used to collect volatile information. It presents a portable forensic environment, which provides access to many Windows based tools.

- Access Pass View is an application available in Windows Live side of the Helix. This application is used to reveal the database password of the password-protected MDB files, which are created by Microsoft Access or Jet Database Engine.

- Forensic Server Project (FSP) is application software, which provides a framework to perform forensic data collection from potentially compromised systems and transporting it to a server via the network interface of the system using TCP/IP.

- Messen PassView is application software present in Helix Live for Windows. This software allows the recovery of passwords from numerous instant messenger programs.

- MD5 Checksum Verifier is an application, which is used as a file integrity checker. It uses MD5 algorithm to produce cryptographic hashes. MD5 Checksum Verifier creates checksums of files and verify their integrity.

- Pslist is a command, which is used to display process, CPU, and memory information or thread statistics for all processes that are running presently on the system.

- Fport is a tool that is used to identify unknown open ports and their associated applications. It reports all open TCP/IP applications and maps them to the owning application. It not only shows the open ports and their status but also maps them to the running processes with their PID, process name, and path.

- Word Extractor is an application, which is used to extract human understandable interpretation from the binary computer files. Word Extractor tool can be used with any file present in the computer.

- When Windows crashes, it creates a memory dump file. This file contains valuable information, which is used to investigate why the system stopped. System requires paging file of at least 2 MB on the boot volume to produce memory dump.

- System state backup is a backup of a complete system, which ensures that no data or information is lost when there is a system crash, a driver file get corrupted, or a system file stops functioning properly.

- Alternate Data Streams (ADS) is a feature of NTFS file system, which allows more than one data stream to be associated with a filename.

- Word Extractor is an application, which is used to extract human understandable interpretation from the binary computer files. Word Extractor tool can be used with any file present in the computer. It separates the strings that contain human text / words from binary code (like applications, DLLs). Features of Word Extractor are as follows:

  i. It replaces non-understandable words with spaces or dots for better understanding.

  ii. It supports drag and drop and wrap text.

  iii. It saves results in a TXT or RTF format.

  iv. It does not thwart registry or system with unwanted DLL files.

- RFC 3227 is a list, which specifies the order of volatility of data in a Windows based system. This list is used to collect volatile data and evidences in a particular order to avoid any error in collection of electronic evidences. The data sources in order of their volatility as given by RFC 3227 are as follows:

    i. Registers, cache

    ii. Routing table, ARP cache, process table, kernel statistics

    iii. Memory

    iv. Temporary file systems

    v. disk

    vi. Remote logging and monitoring data

    vii. Physical configuration, network topology

    viii. Archival media

- There are a number of locations present in Windows host, which acts as a rich source of electronic evidences. Some of the important sources of electronic evidence on a Windows host are as follows:

    i. Files

    ii. Slack space

    iii. Swap files

    iv. Unallocated clusters

    v. Unused partition

    vi. Hidden partition

Pop Quiz

Q1: Which of the following values contains the correct NULL SID string value?

Ans: S-1-0-0

Q2: Which of the following Windows Registry key contains the password file of the user?

Ans: HKEY_LOCAL_MACHINE

Commands and Different Kits of Linux Forensics.

- A loop-back device, vnd (vnode disk), or lofi (loopback file interface) is a pseudo-device in Linux operating systems, which makes a file accessible as a block device. A loop device must be connected to an existing file in the file system. The association provides the user with an API that allows the file to be used in place of a block special file. Thus, if the file contains an entire file system, the file may then be mounted as if it were a disk device.

- In Linux booting sequence, the flow of control is from BIOS, to boot loader, to kernel. The kernel then starts the scheduler (to allow multi-tasking) and runs first userland (i.e. outside kernel space) program Init (which sets up the user environment and allows user interaction and login). At this point the kernel goes idle unless called externally. Linux kernel image is contained in the boot directory (/boot). Either LILO or GRUB may be queried then, by inspection of their configuration files. After this, Linux boot process starts initialization. The file/sbin/init starts the initialization process.

- The Autopsy is a digital forensic browser, which provides graphical interface to The Sleuth Kit. It is an open source digital forensic tool, which runs on UNIX systems. The Autopsy forensic browser interfaces with the command line tools to simplify the process. Autopsy provides many evidence search functionality, which are as follows:

i. File Listing

ii. Hash Database

iii. File Type Sorting

iv. Timeline of File Activity

v. Keyword Search

vi. Meta Data Analysis

- Autopsy also provides number of functions that aid in case management, which are as follows:

i. Event Sequencer

ii. Image Integrity

iii. Reports

iv. Logging

- In the Linux system, permissions are held by three types of users, i.e., the owner of the file, the group belonging to that owner, and other users.

- Set user ID is the Linux access permission flag bit that allows users to run an executable file as the permissions of the executable's owner. When the Set user ID (SUID) bit is set and a user executes the file, the user will have the same rights as the owner.

- The passwd -u and usermod -U commands can be used to unlock a locked user account.

- In the Linux operating system, the /sbin directory contains administrative commands and daemon processes.

- You can retrieve information whether the Linux operating system is in promiscuous mode or not. Such information can be retrieved by using ifconfig | grep PROMISC, searching the log files using the grep Promisc /var/log/messages or using the ip link command.

- The chmod 764 command is used to give all permissions to the owner, Read and Write permissions to groups, and Read Only permissions to other users.

- "/dev" directory in Linux operating system contains device files, which refers to physical devices. Linux treats all devices connected to the computer as a file. These files give direct privilege to forensic analyst to access hardware devices and redirect both input and output to the device.

- "/sbin" directory contains local software, system libraries, games, and other applications. This directory is mounted on separate partition.

- Linux kernel can support a large number of file system.

- "/etc/sbin/init" file starts the initialization process in booting sequence of the Linux operating system. The 'Init' process executes scripts, which is needed to set up all non-operating system services and structures in order to allow a user environment to be created, and then presents the user with a login screen.

- icat command in the Sleuth Kit is used to extract the data units of a file, which is specified by its meta-data address.

- The Autopsy is a digital forensic browser, which provides graphical interface to The Sleuth Kit. It is an open source digital forensic tool, which runs on UNIX systems.

- Squid supports SSL, extensive access controls, and full request logging.

- The sshd_config file is used to control the behavior of the SSH server.

- The w command displays currently logged-in users and their tasks.

- The find /-perm -4000 command searches the current directory and its sub-directories for all the files on which SUID has been set.

Tools for Computer Forensic and Hardware Forensic Tools.

- Device Seizure is a software, which is used in forensic analysis and recovery of mobile phone and PDA data. It is used for data recovery, full data dumps of certain cell phone models, logical and physical acquisitions of PDAs, data cable access, and advanced reporting. Device Seizure also provides feature of GSM SIM card acquisition and deleted data recovery using SIMCon technology.

- Forensic Sorter is software, which is used to organize the contents of a hard drive. It sorts files of hard drive into different categories, such as video, audio, spreadsheets etc. Forensic Sorter also recovers deleted files, or file fragments in slack. It supports drive image in RAW, PFR, safeback, and Encase image file formats. Forensic Sorter sorts file on the basis of their header for more accuracy.

- The Sleuth Kit (TSK) is a library and collection of Unix- and Windows-based tools and utilities to allow for the forensic analysis of computer systems. TSK can be used to perform investigations and data extraction from images of Windows, Linux and Unix computers. The Sleuth Kit is normally used in conjunction with its custom front-end application, Autopsy, to provide a user friendly interface. Now there is a new front-end extended interface named PTK. Several other tools also use TSK for file extraction. The Sleuth Kit is a free, open source suite that provides a large number of specialized command-line based utilities.

- Visual TimeAnalyzer is a software, which is used to track computer activities, working time, pauses, projects, costs, software, and Internet use automatically. It shows detailed, illustrated reports of the activities. Visual TimeAnalyzer also tells which programs were used for how long, when, and by whom. It gives parents control over their children's use of the computer. Visual TimeAnalyzer software has privacy safeguards. It does not monitor all user data such as passwords and personal documents, and does not record specific keystrokes or run screen captures as a background process.

- DriveSpy is a modified MS-DOS shell, which is designed to use standard commands of MS-DOS for forensic purposes.

It uses a set of standard MS-DOS commands followed by commands specific to process the computer during investigations. It can clean an entire drive or partition, unallocated space, or slack space. DriveSpy can also create an MD5 hash of an entire drive, partition, or selected files. It saves and restores compressed images of a partition for forensic use.

- Ontrack is a data recovery tool, which is used to recover lost and deleted data. It provides file repair capability for files in Microsoft Word and Zip format. Ontrack also recovers deleted files, folders, and entire partitions. It uses an emergency boot disks to collect data from systems that cannot boot Windows operating system. The user can configure the filter of the file for a full scan. Ontrack can also filter data according to the different file parameters, such as date, time, name, size, etc.

- ImageMASSter Solo-3 is a forensic data acquisition tool, which is used to capture data and make images of the hard drives. It can capture data from IDE, Serial ATA, SCSI drives, and flash cards. ImageMASSter Solo-3 can generates MD5 and CRC32 hashes during the data capture. It can acquire data with a transfer rate up to 3 GB/minute and has a touch screen user interface.

- A cyclic redundancy check (CRC) is a non-secure hash function designed to detect accidental changes to raw computer data, and commonly used in digital networks and storage devices such as hard disk drives. A CRC-enabled device calculates a short, fixed-length binary sequence, known as the CRC code or just CRC, for each block of data and sends or stores them both together. When a block is read or received the device repeats the calculation; if the new CRC does not match the one calculated earlier, then the block contains a data error and the device may take corrective action such as rereading or requesting the block be sent again.

- The ImageMASSter 4002i is the tool, which is used for forensic investigations. It is used to duplicate P-ATA and S-ATA drives of high volume. ImageMASSter 4002i copies two drives simultaneously at speed up to 2GB/min.

Multiple Copy Modes are also available in ImageMASSter 4002i to support the Windows and non-Windows operating Systems. Partitions are scaled and formatted during the copy process, eliminating the requirement of manual preparation of a drive before usage. The ImageMASSter 4002i is also equipped with the Wipeout option, which provides a quick method for erasing data from hard drives.

- The Wipe MASSter is a hardware forensic tool, which is used to erase data of the hard drives. It can erase data of nine drives simultaneously at speed up to 3GB/min. The Wipe MASSter is also used to perform high volume hard drive sanitizing operations using P-ATA, S-ATA and laptop hard drives by using optional adapters. The Wipe MASSter can erase data of hard drives of different sizes and models in the same operation. It is also provided with an option for formatting the sanitized drives.

- FireWire DriveDock is a forensic instrument, which is designed to load hard drives on computer systems. It is attached with the hard drives using FireWire 400 or USB cables. It also has dual FireWire 400 ports, which allow daisy-chaining for more efficiency. FireWire DriveDock does not require any additional drivers. It can transfer data at the transfer rate of minimum 35 MB per second.Group policy object (GPO) is a collection of group policy settings. It can be created using a Windows utility known as the Group Policy snap-in. GPO affects the user and computer accounts located in sites, domains, and organizational units (OUs).

- Device Seizure is a software, which is used in forensic analysis and recovery of mobile phone and PDA data. It is used for data recovery, full data dumps of certain cell phone models, logical and physical acquisitions of PDAs, data cable access, and advanced reporting.

- Forensic Sorter is a software, which is used to organize the contents of a hard drive. It sorts files in hard drive in different categories, such as video, audio, spreadsheets etc. Forensic Sorter also recovers deleted files, or file fragments in slack.

- Visual TimeAnalyzer is a software, which is used to track computer activities, working time, pauses, projects, costs, software, and Internet use automatically.

- DriveSpy is a modified MS-DOS shell, which is designed to use standard commands of MS-DOS for forensic purposes. It uses a set of standard MS-DOS commands followed by commands specific to process the computer during investigations.

- ImageMASSter Solo-3 is a forensic data acquisition tool, which is used to capture data and make images of the hard drives. It can capture data from IDE, Serial ATA, SCSI drives, and flash cards. ImageMASSter Solo-3 can generates MD5 and CRC32 hashes during the data capture.

Methods of Investigating using Encase.

- EnCase is a series of proprietary forensic software products produced by Guidance Software. It is used by many law enforcement agencies and corporations around the world to support civil/criminal investigations, network investigations, data compliance and electronic discovery. EnCase is designed to make forensic quality recordings of data stored on PCs, and to recover some insecurely deleted data. The network-enabled version of EnCase is capable of taking snapshots of RAM over time on a target computer. Special training is usually required to operate the software in a law enforcement capacity.

Pop Quiz

Q1: Which utility is used to view information about logged in users in Linux?

Ans:finger

Q2: Which forensic tool suite is developed for Linux operating system?

Ans: S.M.A.R.T.

- HAVAL is a cryptographic hash function. Unlike MD5, but like most modern cryptographic hash functions, HAVAL can produce hashes of different lengths. HAVAL can produce hashes in lengths of 128 bits, 160 bits, 192 bits, 224 bits, and 256 bits. HAVAL also allows users to specify the number of rounds (3, 4, or 5) to be used to generate the hash.

- The host protected area (HPA), sometimes referred to as hidden protected area, is an area of a hard drive that is not normally visible to an operating system (OS). It is an area of the disk, which is hidden from the BIOS. HPA contains data such as vendor restoration utilities. HPA can be used to store data that is deemed illegal and is thus of interest to government and police computer forensics teams. HPA is also used by various theft recovery and monitoring service vendors.

- MD5 and CRC cryptographic methods are used in EnCase forensic software to ensure the integrity of the data.

- Secure Authentication for EnCase (SAFE) method is used by forensic investigators to acquire an image over the network in a secure manner.

- Linux hard disk naming convention is the method of assigning name to the different storage media attached to the computer

- An administrative template can be used to specify the options available for setting the group policy.

Key Terms

RFC	Request for Comments
IETF	Internet Engineering Task Force
FAU	Forensic Acquisition Utilities

Test Your Knowledge

Q1.   Sandra, a novice computer user, works on Windows environment. She experiences some problem regarding bad sectors formed in a hard disk of her computer. She wants to run CHKDSK command to check the hard disk for bad sectors and to fix the errors, if any, occurred. Which of the following switches will she use with CHKDSK command to accomplish the task?

   A.   CHKDSK /V /X

   B.   CHKDSK /R /F

   C.   CHKDSK /I

   D.   CHKDSK /C /L

Q2.   Adam works as a professional Computer Hacking Forensic Investigator, a project has been assigned to him to investigate and examine files present on suspect's computer. Adam uses a tool with the help of which he can examine recovered deleted files, fragmented files, and other corrupted data. He can also examine the data, which was captured from the network, and access the physical RAM, and any processes running in virtual memory with the help of this tool. Which of the following tools is Adam using?

   A.   WinHex

   B.   Evidor

   C.   Vedit

   D.   HxD

Q3.   Adam works as a professional Computer Hacking Forensic Investigator. A project has been assigned to him to investigate computer of an unfaithful employee of SecureEnet Inc. Suspect's computer runs on Windows operating system. Which of the following sources will Adam investigate on a Windows host to collect the electronic evidences?

Each correct answer represents a complete solution. Choose all that apply.

A.   Slack spaces

B.   Swap files

C.   Allocated cluster

D.   Unused and hidden partition

Q4. Which of the following data is NOT listed as a volatile data in RFC 3227 list for Windows based system?

A Routing table

B Temporary file system

C Data on a hard disk

D Kernel statistics

Q5. Which of the following command line tools are available in Helix Live acquisition tool on Windows?

Each correct answer represents a complete solution. Choose all that apply.

A.   .cab extractors

B.   ipconfig

C.   netstat

D.   whois

Answer Explanation

A1.   Answer option B is correct.

Sandra will use CHKDSK /R /F command to accomplish the task. CHKDSK /R /F command is used to locate the bad sectors and any readable information, which can be recovered. It is also used to fix any errors found.

Answer options A, C, and D are incorrect. All these switches will not give the required result.

A2.   Answer option A is correct.

According to the scenario Adam is using WinHex hexadecimal editor tool. WinHex is a famous hexadecimal editor tool that is used to examine files that have been collected for analysis and examination. This includes file fragments, recovered deleted files, or other data that have been corrupted or destroyed. WinHex can also examine the contents of a file retrieved from a hard disk whose application software, which open the particular file, is not available. We can also view data captured from a network to identify passwords and other data. WinHex also provides a feature that allows cloning of a hard disk and thus making a duplicate of the data to work with. It can also provide a RAM editor feature that allows access to the physical RAM and any processes running in virtual memory. WinHex is also set to run in a write-protected mode, which open any file in a read-only mode to prevent any modification in the original data.

Answer options B, C, and D are incorrect. All these tools cannot be used.

A3.   Answer options A, B, and D are correct.

There are a number of locations present in Windows host, which acts as a rich source of electronic evidences. Some of the important sources of electronic evidence on a Windows host are as follows:

- Files

- Slack space

- Swap files

- Unallocated clusters

- Unused partition

- Hidden partition

Answer option C is incorrect. This is not the valid source of electronic evidence.

A4. Answer option C is correct.

Data on a hard disk is not included as a volatile memory in the RFC 3227 list. RFC 3227 is a list, which specifies the order of volatility of data in a Windows based system. This list is used to collect volatile data and evidences in a particular order to avoid any error in collection of electronic evidences. The data sources in order of their volatility as given by RFC 3227 are as follows:

- Registers, cache

- Routing table, ARP cache, process table, kernel statistics

- Memory

- Temporary file systems

- disk

- Remote logging and monitoring data

- Physical configuration, network topology

- Archival media

A5. Answer options A, B, and C are correct.

All these command-line tools are available in Helix Live acquisition tool on Windows. Helix is a live acquisition tool, which is used to collect volatile information. It presents a portable forensic environment, which provides access to many Windows based tools. Helix contains static binaries for Linux, Solaris and Windows using GNU utilities and Cygwin tools. These tools include Sysinternal's tools, Garners Forensic Acquisition Utilities suite, Windows Toolchest, and Windows Debugger. One of the important advantages of Helix tool is that it maintains the integrity of command line by ensuring that Windows built in command line tools do not run from the compromised system. Windows command-line tools present in Helix are as follows:

- cab extractor

- ipconfig

- kill

- netstat

- Process explorer

Answer option D is incorrect. This command line tool is not present in Helix.

Chapter 5 - Data acquisition and Duplication, Recovering Deleted Files and Partition.

Overview

Data acquisition (abbreviated DAQ) is the process of sampling of real world physical conditions and conversion of the resulting samples into digital numeric values that can be manipulated by a computer. Data acquisition and data acquisition systems (abbreviated with the acronym DAS) typically involves the conversion of analog waveforms into digital values for processing.

The system partition is a disk partition that contains the boot sector and files such as NTLDR that are needed for booting Windows XP and earlier.

The boot partition is the disk partition that contains the Windows operating system files and its support files, but not any files responsible for booting.

The system partition can be different from the boot partition, although they are often on the same partition (drive C:). Windows setup places the initial system partition based on motherboard BIOS settings. Bitlocker requires a separate, unencrypted system partition for booting.

The master boot record is located at physical sector 0, just before the partition table, and is therefore not contained inside any of the logical partitions or volumes.

It is interesting to note that in operating systems other than Windows and DOS the definitions of boot partition and system partition are just the opposite: the boot partition contains the boot files and the system partitions hold the operating system files.

Key Points

Software and Hardware Tools for Data Acquisition and Duplication.

- File slack is the space, which exists on a Windows disk between the end of file and the end of the last cluster. It can contain data from the memory of the system.

- File slack is very useful for Forensic Investigators, as it may be possible to find user names, passwords, and other important information related to the system in the file slack. Large cluster size will increase the volume of the file slack leading to the wastage of storage space.

Pop Quiz

Q1: Which tools is used to locate lost files and partitions to restore data from a formatted, damaged, or lost partition in Windows and Apple Macintosh computers?

Ans: VirtualLab

Q2: Which of the following tools is used to create a backup of the first physical disk and partitions on the computer?

Ans: PC ParaChute

- Timbersee and Swatch are tools used for logging network activities in the Linux operating system.

- File slack is the space, which exists in Windows disk between the end of file and the end of the last cluster. It can contain data from the memory of the system.

- A firewall analyzes all the traffic between a network and the Internet, and provides centralized access control on how users should use the network.

Concept of File Deletion and Damaged Files.

- del (or erase) is a command in various DOS, OS/2 and Microsoft Windows command line interpreters (shells) such as COMMAND.COM, cmd.exe, 4DOS/4NT and Windows PowerShell. It is used to delete one or more files or directories from a file system. It is analogous to the Unix rm command. RT-11, RSX-11 and OpenVMS also provide the delete command which can be contracted to del. In Windows PowerShell, del and erase are a predefined command aliases for the Remove-Item Cmdlet, which basically serves the same purpose.

Pop Quiz

Q1: What is the name of the folder which stores deleted files in Windows Vista?

Ans: Recycle.Bin

Q2: Which of the following tools is used to access deleted file in Windows environment?

Ans: Active@ UNERASER

- del (or erase) command is used with different switches, which are as follows:

Switch	Description
/p	It prompts you for confirmation as to whether you want to delete the file.
/f	It forces the deletion of read-only files.
/s	It deletes the specified files from the current directory and any sub-directories.
/q	It specifies not to prompt for confirmation before deleting files. This is called quiet mode.
/ar	It deletes read-only files.
/aa	It deletes archive files.
/as	It deletes system files.
/ah	It deletes hidden files.

- IPTables is a firewall that is a replacement of the IPChains firewall for the Linux 2.4 kernel and later versions.

- A SQL injection attack is a process in which an attacker tries to execute unauthorized SQL statements via inputting malicious SQL queries and wild characters.

- The "nmap -v -O target_address" command is used for OS fingerprinting.

- Del (or erase) command is used to delete one or more files or directories from a file system.

Partition Recovery Tools and Method.

- Undelete is a command-line tool that is used on the old systems, allowing a user to simply type UNDELETE followed by the path to the file the user wish to restore.

- If the user wanted to undelete a file named text.txt from your root directory, the user simply type UNDELETE C:\TEXT.TXT. This command will restore the file.

- Active@ UNDELETE is data recovery software that is used to recover data from basic and dynamic volumes, including RAID volumes, and hard disks more than 500 GB. It also supports recovery from removable storage devices, such as USB flash drives, ZIP drives, and memory sticks and cards.

- Active@ UNERASER is a data recovery tool that runs on Windows or DOS. With the help of this tool a user can access deleted files before the booting of Windows. It supports local files, compressed files, MBR backups. Active@ UNERASER can also access the sectors of the disk drive with a disk viewer feature. This tool can run from either a bootable floppy disk or a CD.

- R-Undelete is a tool that is used to restore deleted files. It also provides an easy-to-use wizard, which takes a user through the steps of recovering a file. R-Undelete also provides features that allow the user to reconstruct damaged graphics, audio, and video files.

- Restoration is a tool that was originally written by Brian Kato. It is a fast and easy, which is small enough to run from a floppy disk. It allows a user not only to view any deleted files on a hard disk but also to search for specific files by entering all or part of the filename into a search box.

Pop Quiz

Q1: Which of the following commands is used to create or delete partitions on Windows XP?

Ans: DISKPARTr

Q2: Which of the following tools is used to recover data and partitions, and can run on Windows, Linux, SunOS, and Macintosh OS X operating systems?

Ans: TestDisk

Test Your Knowledge

Q1. Which of the following statements is NOT true about the file slack spaces in Windows operating system?

    A.   File slack is the space, which exists between the end of the file and the end of the last cluster.

    B.   It is possible to find user names, passwords, and other important information in slack.

    C.   File slack may contain data from the memory of the system.

    D.   Large cluster size will decrease the volume of the file slack.

Q2. Which of the following functions are performed by a firewall?

Each correct answer represents a complete solution. Choose all that apply.

    A.   It blocks unwanted traffic.

    B.   It hides vulnerable computers that are exposed to the Internet.

    C.   It logs traffic to and from the private network.

    D.   It enhances security through various methods, including packet filtering, circuit-level filtering, and application filtering.

Q3. A firewall is a combination of hardware and software, used to provide security to a network. It is used to protect an internal network or intranet against unauthorized access from the Internet or other outside networks. It restricts inbound and outbound access and can analyze all traffic between an internal network and the Internet. Users can configure a firewall to pass or block packets from specific IP addresses and ports. Which of the following tools works as a firewall for the Linux 2.4 kernel?

    A.   IPChains

B.   IPTables

C.   Stunnel

D.   OpenSSH

Q4. John works as a professional Ethical Hacker. He is assigned a project to test the security of www.we-are-secure.com. He enters a single quote in the input field of the login page of the We-are-secure Web site and receives the following error message:

Microsoft OLE DB Provider for ODBC Drivers error '0x80040E14'

This error message shows that the We-are-secure Website is vulnerable to _____.

A.   An XSS attack

B.   A Denial-of-Service attack

C.   A buffer overflow

D.   A SQL injection attack

Q5. John works as a contract Ethical Hacker. He has recently got a project to do security checking for www.we-are-secure.com. He wants to find out the operating system of the we-are-secure server in the information gathering step. Which of the following commands will he use to accomplish the task?

Each correct answer represents a complete solution. Choose two.

A.   nmap -v -O 208.100.2.25

B.   nc -v -n 208.100.2.25 80

C.   nc 208.100.2.25 23

D.   nmap -v -O www.we-are-secure.com

Answer Explanation

A1.   Answer option C is correct.

File slack is the space, which exists on a Windows disk between the end of file and the end of the last cluster. It can contain data from the memory of the system. File slack is very useful for Forensic Investigators, as it may be possible to find user names, passwords, and other important information related to the system in the file slack. Large cluster size will increase the volume of the file slack leading to the wastage of storage space.

Answer options A, B, and D are incorrect. All these statements are true about the file slack.

A2.   Answer options A, B, C, and D are correct.

A firewall is a combination of software and hardware that prevents data packets from coming in or going out of a specified network or computer. It is used to separate an internal network from the Internet. It analyzes all the traffic between a network and the Internet, and provides centralized access control on how users should use the network. A firewall can also perform the following functions:

- Block unwanted traffic.

- Direct the incoming traffic to more trustworthy internal computers.

- Hide vulnerable computers that are exposed to the Internet.

- Log traffic to and from the private network.

A3.   Answer option B is correct.

IPTables is a firewall that is a replacement of the IPChains firewall for the Linux 2.4 kernel and later versions.

Answer option A is incorrect. IPChains is a linux packet filtering firewall that allows a Network Administrator to ACCEPT, DENY, MASQ, or REDIRECT packets.

Answer option C is incorrect. Stunnel is an SSL wrapper that allows a Network Administrator to encrypt an arbitrary TCP connection inside the Secure Socket Layer (SSL) protocol. Stunnel can be also used to secure non-SSL daemons and protocols, e.g., POP3, IMAP, NNTP, LDAP, etc. It is available for both the Windows and Linux operating systems.

Answer option D is incorrect. Open Secure Shell (OpenSSH) is an application that provides secure encrypted communication between two untrusted hosts over a network. It provides secure tunneling and several authentication methods, and supports all SSH protocol versions.

A4.   Answer option D is correct.

This error message shows that the We-are-secure server is using a Microsoft SQL server database and the programmer has not filtered the Web site for a SQL injection attack well. A SQL injection attack is the process in which an attacker tries to execute unauthorized SQL statements by inputting malicious SQL queries and wild characters. These statements can be used to delete data from a database, as well as database objects such as tables, views, stored procedures, etc. An attacker can either directly enter the code into input variables or insert malicious code in strings that can be stored in a database.

Answer option A is incorrect. An XSS (cross site scripting) attack is a computer security exploit that occurs when a Web application is used to gather data from a victim.

Answer option B is incorrect. A Denial-of-Service (DoS) attack is mounted with the objective of causing a negative impact on the performance of a computer or network. It is also known as a network saturation attack or bandwidth consumption attack. Attackers perform DoS attacks by sending a large number of protocol packets to the network. The effects of a DoS attack are as follows:

- Saturates network resources

- Disrupts connections between two computers, thereby preventing communications between services

- Disrupts services to a specific computer

- Causes failure to access a Web site

- Results in an increase in the amount of spam

A Denial-of-Service attack is very common on the Internet because it is much easier to accomplish. Most of the DoS attacks rely on the weaknesses in the TCP/IP protocol.

Answer option C is incorrect. Buffer overflow is a condition in which an application receives more data than it is configured to accept. It helps an attacker not only to execute a malicious code on the target system but also to install backdoors on the target system for further attacks. All buffer overflow attacks are due to only sloppy programming or poor memory management by the application developers. The main types of buffer overflows are:

- Stack overflow

- Format string overflow

- Heap overflow

- Integer overflow

A5.   Answer options A and D are correct.

According to the scenario, John will use "nmap -v -O 208.100.2.25" to detect the operating system of the we-are-secure server. Here, -v is used for verbose and -O is used for TCP/IP fingerprinting to guess the remote operating system.

John may also use the DNS name of we-are-secure instead of using the IP address of the we-are-secure server. So, he can also use the nmap command "nmap-v-Owww.we-are-secure.com".

Answer option B is incorrect. "nc -v -n 208.100.2.25 80" is a Netcat command, which is used to banner grab for getting information about the services running on any port.

Answer option C is incorrect. "nc 208.100.2.25 23" is a Netcat command, which is used to listen to a port for incoming connections.

Chapter 6 - Image File Forensics, Steganography, Application Password Crackers

Overview

Image file formats is standardized means of organizing and storing images. Image files are composed of either pixel or vector (geometric) data that are rasterized to pixels when displayed (with few exceptions) in a vector graphic display. The pixels that constitute an image are ordered as a grid (columns and rows); each pixel consists of numbers representing magnitudes of brightness and color.

Key Points

Understanding different Image File Formats.

- JPEG-compressed images are usually stored in the JFIF (JPEG File Interchange Format) file format.

- JPEG compression is lossy compression. The JPEG/JFIF filename extension in DOS is JPG (other operating systems may use JPEG).

- The Exif (Exchangeable image file format) format is a file standard similar to the JFIF format with TIFF extensions; it is incorporated in the JPEG-writing software used in most cameras. Its purpose is to record and to standardize the exchange of images with image metadata between digital cameras and editing and viewing software.

- The TIFF (Tagged Image File Format) format is a flexible format that normally saves 8 bits or 16 bits per color (red, green, blue) for 24-bit and 48-bit totals, respectively, usually using either the TIFF or TIF filename extension.

- The PNG (Portable Network Graphics) file format was created as the free, open-source successor to the GIF. The PNG file format supports truecolor (16 million colors) while the GIF supports only 256 colors. The PNG file excels when the image has large, uniformly colored areas.

- GIF (Graphics Interchange Format) is limited to an 8-bit palette, or 256 colors. This makes the GIF format suitable for storing graphics with relatively few colors such as simple diagrams, shapes, logos and cartoon style images.

- Netpbm format is a family including the portable pixmap file format (PPM), the portable graymap file format (PGM) and the portable bitmap file format (PBM). These are either pure ASCII files or raw binary files with an ASCII header that provide very basic functionality and serve as a lowest-common-denominator for converting pixmap, graymap, or bitmap files between different platforms.

Pop Quiz

Q1: Which image file formats uses a lossy data compression technique?

Ans: JPG

Q2: Which tool is used for disk encryption?

Ans: WinMagic SecureDoc

- CGM (Computer Graphics Metafile) is a file format for 2D vector graphics, raster graphics, and text, and is defined by ISO/IEC 8632. All graphical elements can be specified in a textual source file that can be compiled into a binary file or one of two text representations. CGM provides a means of graphics data interchange for computer representation of 2D graphical information independent from any particular application, system, platform, or device.

- SVG (Scalable Vector Graphics) is an open standard created and developed by the World Wide Web Consortium to address the need (and attempts of several corporations) for a versatile, scriptable and all-purpose vector format for the web and otherwise.

Steganalysis

- There are many tools and methods available for Steganography attack. These tools are used to recover the hidden information from the image file.

- Snow.exe is a Steganography tool that is used to hide secret data within text files. It is based on the concept that spaces and tabs are generally not visible in text viewers and therefore a message can be effectively hidden without affecting the text's visual representation for the casual observer.

- Steganography is the art and science of writing hidden messages in such a way that no one, apart from the sender and intended recipient, is able to detect the presence of information. There are various methods available to accomplish Steganography.

- An Active Attack is a type of Steganography attack in which the attacker changes the carrier during the communication process. It is also known as Disabling attack. A number of techniques are used in this attack.

- Blur technique is used for smoothing the transition and controlling contrast on the hard edges, where there is significant color transition.

- Noise Reduction technique is used to reduce the noise by adjusting color and averaging pixel values. Noise is rectified by insertion of random or uniform pixels and colors, which resemble to the original pixels.

- Sharpen technique is used to increase color contrast between adjacent pixels at the edges of objects.

- Rotate technique is used to rotate an image in any direction around its centre point in a given space.

- Resample technique is used to expand an image to large size thus decreasing ruggedness.

- Soften technique is a type of Blur with the difference that it applies a uniform blur to smooth edges and reduce contrast.

- Steganography is the art and science of hiding information by embedding harmful messages within other seemingly harmless messages. It works by replacing bits of unused data in regular computer files, such as graphics, sound, text, and HTML, with bits of invisible information.

- Dskprobe is a tool that is used to detect steganography.

- Stealth is a tool used for performing steganography in PGP files. It strips off identifying information from the header, after which PGP files can be used for steganography.

Different Attacks and Tools of Steganography

- Watermarking is the irreversible process of embedding information in to a digital media. The purpose of digital watermarks is to provide copyright protection for intellectual property that is in digital form.

- Visible watermarking, data or information is clearly visible on the picture or on the video. Generally this type of watermarking is used to identify the owner of the media and to enforce the copyright. It also serves the purpose of advertisement.

- Invisible watermarking, information is added in a hidden form to the digital media. One of the major applications of invisible watermarking is to prevent unauthorized copying of digital media.

- 2Mosaic is a tool used for watermark breaking. It is an attack against a digital watermarking system. In this type of attack, an image is chopped into small pieces and then placed together. When this image is embedded into a web page, the web browser renders the small pieces into one image. This image looks like a real image with no watermark in it. This attack is successful, as it is impossible to read watermark in very small pieces.

- Steganographic file system is a technique of storing files in such a manner that it encrypts data and hide it in a efficient way so that it cannot be traced.

- Imagehide and Snow.exe are steganography tools.

- Sam Spade, WsPingPro, and SuperScan can be used to perform a whois query.

- Watermarking is the process of embedding information in the digital media that serves the purpose of protecting copyright system. Digital Watermarking is vulnerable to some attacks. These attacks are used to get rid of the digital watermark from the images.

Password Cracking Tools and Attacks

- The rainbow attack is the fastest method of password cracking. This method of password cracking is implemented by calculating all the possible hashes for a set of characters and then storing them in a table known as the Rainbow table. These password hashes are then employed to the tool that uses the Rainbow algorithm and searches the Rainbow table until the password is not fetched.

- A rule-based password cracking attack is employed when the attacker gets some information about the password, generally some form of documents describing password policies of a certain organization. By obtaining useful information (such as the length of password, use of numbers and special characters etc.), the attacker can easily adjust and optimize the cracking tool to retrieve passwords.

- John the Ripper is a fast password cracker available for various environments. Its primary purpose is to detect weak Unix/Linux passwords. Initially developed for the Unix operating system, it currently runs on fifteen different platforms. It is one of the most popular password testing/breaking programs, as it combines a number of password crackers into one package. It can be run against various encrypted password formats including several crypt password hash types most commonly found on various Unix platforms.

- Ophcrack is an open source program that cracks Windows passwords by using LM hashes through rainbow tables. The program includes the ability to import the hashes from a variety of formats, including dumping directly from the SAM files of Windows. These tables can crack 99.9% of alphanumeric passwords of up to 14 characters in usually a few minutes. Ophcrack also cracks NTLM hashes. This is necessary if the generation of the LM hash is disabled (this is default for Windows Vista), or if the password is longer than 14 characters (in which case the LM hash is not stored).

- The meet-in-the-middle attack is a cryptographic attack which, like the birthday attack, makes use of a space-time tradeoff. While the birthday attack attempts to find two values in the domain of a function that map to the same value in its range. The meet-in-the-middle attack attempts to find a value in each of the ranges and domains of the composition of two functions such that the forward mapping of one through the first function is the same as the inverse image of the other through the second function.

- TCPflow is a program, which is used to capture the data transmitted as part of TCP connections, and stores the data in a way that is convenient for protocol analysis or debugging. This program uses other programs like 'tcpdump' to show a summary of packets seen on the network. TCPflow reconstructs the actual data streams and stores each flow in a separate file for later analysis.

- When an attacker performs a dictionary as well as a brute force attack, the attack is known as a hybrid attack. In this method, an attack is performed with the dictionary attack method of adding numerals and symbols to dictionary words.

- In a brute force attack, an attacker uses software that tries a large number of the keys combinations in order to get a password. To prevent such attacks, users should create passwords more difficult to guess, e.g., using a minimum of six characters, alphanumeric combinations, and lower-upper case combinations, etc.

- Dictionary attack is a type of password guessing attack. This type of attack uses a dictionary of common words to find out the password of a user. It can also use common words in either upper or lower case to find a password. There are many programs available on the Internet to automate and execute dictionary attacks.

- Man-in-the-middle attacks occur when an attacker successfully inserts an intermediary software or program between two communicating hosts. The intermediary software or program allows attackers to listen to and modify the communication packets passing between the two hosts. The software intercepts the communication packets and then sends the information to the receiving host. The receiving host responds to the software, presuming it to be the legitimate client.

- Replay attack is a type of attack in which attackers capture packets containing passwords or digital signatures whenever packets pass between two hosts on a network. In an attempt to obtain an authenticated connection, the attackers then resend the captured packet to the system. In this type of attacks, the attacker does not know the actual password, but can simply replay the captured packet.

- Pwdump is a password cracker that outputs the LM and NTLM password hashes of local user accounts from the Security Account Manager (SAM), regardless of whether Syskey is enabled. It can also display password histories if they are available and outputs the data in L0phtcrack-compatible form. However, in order to work, it must be run under an Administrator account, or be able to access an Administrator account on the computer where the hashes are to be dumped; so pwdump does not compromise security.

- Password Authentication Protocol (PAP) is the least sophisticated authentication protocol, used mostly when a client calls a server running an operating system other than Windows. PAP uses plain text passwords.

- Brutus can be used to perform brute force attacks, dictionary attacks, or hybrid attacks.

- Password cracking attack is the most important and dangerous threat to the security of a user. There are various methods of password cracking, each one of them having unique set of rules and algorithm to complete the task.

- Rainbow attack is the fastest method of password cracking. This method of password cracking is implemented by calculating all the possible hashes for a set of characters and then storing them in a table known as the Rainbow table.

- PAP uses plain text passwords.

Manage Certificate Revocations

- Online Responder is a trusted server that conveys information about the validity of a certificate. An Online Responder receives and responds only to individual requests from clients regarding information about the status of a certificate. Even if there are many revoked certificates, the Online Responder sends only the data that is requested. This enables the amount of data retrieved to remain low.

Pop Quiz

Q1: Which tool is an asterisk password revealer tool?

Ans: SnadBoy

Q2: which files stores the password in the Linux operating system?

Ans: Shadow

- An Online Responder receives and responds only to individual requests from clients for information about the status of a certificate.

- In public key infrastructures (PKIs) environment, a certificate revocation list (CRL) is a list of certificates that have been revoked or are no longer valid, and therefore should not be relied upon. A CRL is generated and published periodically, after a defined timeframe. A CRL can also be published immediately after a certificate has been revoked. The CRL is always issued by the CA which issues the corresponding certificates.

- Basic Authentication requires a user to provide logon credentials so that only authenticated users are able to access the SMTP virtual server.

Test Your Knowledge

Q1. Which of the following tools is used to hide secret data in text files and is based on the concept that spaces and tabs are generally not visible in text viewers and therefore a message can be effectively hidden without affecting the text's visual representation for the casual observer?

    A.   Image hide

    B.   Snow.exe

    C.   SARA

    D.   Fpipe

Q2. Victor wants to send an encrypted message to his friend. He is using certain steganography technique to accomplish this task. He takes a cover object and changes it accordingly to hide information. This secret information is recovered only when the algorithm compares the changed cover with the original cover. Which of the following Steganography methods is Victor using to accomplish the task?

    A.   The cover generation technique

    B.   The distortion technique

    C.   The spread spectrum technique

    D.   The substitution technique

Q3. John used to work as a Network Administrator for We-are-secure Inc. Now he has resigned from the company for personal reasons. He wants to send out some secret information of the company. To do so, he takes an image file and simply uses a tool **image hide** and embeds the secret file within an image file of the famous actress, Jennifer Lopez, and sends it to his Yahoo mail id. Since he is using the image file to send the data, the mail server of his company is unable to filter this mail. Which of the following techniques is he performing to accomplish his task?

    A.   Web ripping

      B.   Social engineering

      C.   Email spoofing

      D.   Steganography

Q4. Which of the following tools can be used to detect the steganography?

      A.   Dskprobe

      B.   Snow

      C.   Blindside

      D.   ImageHide

Q5. You want to use PGP files for steganography. Which of the following tools will you use to accomplish the task?

      A.   Stealth

      B.   Snow

      C.   Blindside

      D.   ImageHide

Answer Explanation

A1.   Answer option B is correct.

Snow.exe is a Steganography tool that is used to hide secret data in text files. It is based on the concept that spaces and tabs are generally not visible in text viewers and therefore a message can be effectively hidden without affecting the text's visual representation for the casual observer. It achieves this by appending white spaces to the ends of lines in ASCII text.

Answer option A is incorrect. Image hide is a steganography program that hides text within an image. Steganography can encrypt or decrypt malicious data into images that appear identical to the original images. It is estimated that a 640 x 480 pixel image with a color resolution of 256 colors can hide approximately 300KB of information. High resolution images are noted for their payload. For example, a 1024 x 768 pixel image with a 24-bit color resolution can carry about 2.3MB as payload. Image hide warns its users not to save the image file in JPEG format since it is a lossy algorithm and malicious data may be lost during compression.

Answer option C is incorrect. Security Auditor's Research Assistant (SARA) is a third generation Unix-based security analysis tool that supports the FBI Top 20 Consensus on Security. It is an upgrade of the SATAN tool and operates on most UNIX platforms. SARA interfaces with NMAP for OS fingerprinting. The main features of SARA are as follows:

- It is integrated with National Vulnerability Database.

- It supports CVE standards.

- It performs SQL injection tests.

- It is available as a free-use open SATAN-oriented license.

Answer option D is incorrect. Fpipe is a source port forwarder and redirector tool. It can create a TCP or UDP stream with a source port. This tool is useful for finding out the flaws in firewalls that allow traffic through source ports to connect with internal servers. Fpipe works in the same way as Datapipe but is designed to work for Windows operating systems rather than Linux operating systems. For example, if an attacker wants to redirect the TCP port number 80 with the UDP port number 40, the attacker will use the following command:

fpipe -l 80 -r 40 -u destination_IP_addr

A2.   Answer option B is correct.

The distortion technique of steganography creates a change in the cover object to hide the information. This hidden information is recovered by recipient by comparing changed cover with the original cover.

Answer option A is incorrect. The cover generation technique is very similar to the distortion technique. The only difference is that the cover generation method creates a cover for the sole purpose of hiding information rather than changing any existing cover.

Answer option C is incorrect. The spread spectrum method of steganography uses spreading of bandwidth of a narrow band signal across a wide band of frequencies. This technique uses this variation to attach information and send by allocating frequency channel spread across spectrum.

Answer option D is incorrect. The substitution method of steganography uses the wasted and redundant space of digital cover file to hide information on the bit level within the digital cover.

A3.   Answer option D is correct.

According to the scenario, John is performing the Steganography technique for sending malicious data. Steganography is an art and science of hiding information by embedding harmful messages within other seemingly harmless messages. It works by replacing bits of unused data, such as graphics, sound, text, and HTML, with bits of invisible information in regular computer files. This hidden information can be in the form of plain text, cipher text, or even in the form of images.

Answer option A is incorrect. Web ripping is a technique in which the attacker copies the whole structure of a Web site to the local disk and obtains all files of the Web site. Web ripping helps an attacker to trace the loopholes of the Web site.

Answer option B is incorrect. Social engineering is the art of convincing people and making them disclose useful information such as account names and passwords. This information is further exploited by hackers to gain access to a user's computer or network. This method involves mental ability of the people to trick someone rather than their technical skills. A user should always distrust people who ask him for his account name or password, computer name, IP address, employee ID, or other information that can be misused.

Answer option C is incorrect. John is not performing email spoofing. In email spoofing, an attacker sends emails after writing another person's mailing address in the **from field** of the email id.

A4.   Answer option A is correct.

Dskprobe is a tool that is used to detect steganography. Steganography is an art and science of hiding information by embedding harmful messages within other seemingly harmless messages. It works by replacing bits of unused data, such as graphics, sound, text, and HTML, with bits of invisible information in regular computer files. This hidden information can be in the form of plain text, cipher text, or even in the form of images.

Answer options B, C, and D are incorrect. The Snow, Blindside, and ImageHide tools are used to perform steganography.

A5.   Answer option A is correct.

Stealth is a tool used for performing steganography in PGP files. It strips off identifying information from the header, after which PGP files can be used for steganography. Steganography is an art and science of hiding information by embedding harmful messages within other seemingly harmless messages. It works by replacing bits of unused data, such as graphics, sound, text, and HTML, with bits of invisible information in regular computer files. This hidden information can be in the form of plain text, cipher text, or even in the form of images.

Answer options B, C, and D are incorrect. Snow, Blindside, and ImageHide tools are used to perform steganography in an image, not in PGP files.

Chapter 7 - Network Forensics and Investigating logs, Investigating Wireless and Web attacks, Router Forensics.

Overview

A computer network, often simply referred to as a network, is a collection of computers and devices connected by communications channels that facilitates communications among users and allows users to share resources with other users. Networks may be classified according to a wide variety of characteristics.

Key Points

Process and Evidence of Intrusion and Hacking of Network

- The Open Systems Interconnection Model (OSI Model) is an abstract description for layered communications and computer network protocol design. In its most basic form, it divides network architecture into seven layers which, from top to bottom, are the Application, Presentation, Session, Transport, Network, Data-Link, and Physical Layers. A layer is a collection of conceptually similar functions that provide services to the layer above it and receives service from the layer below it.

OSI Model			
	Data unit	**Layer**	**Function**
Host layers	Data	7. Application	Network process to application
		6. Presentation	Data representation and encryption
		5. Session	Interhost communication
	Segment	4. Transport	End-to-end connections and reliability
Media layers	Packet	3. Network	Path determination and logical addressing
	Frame	2. Data Link	Physical addressing
	Bit	1. Physical	Media, signal and binary transmission

- An IP address (Internet Protocol address) is a logical address, which is used for providing a unique identity to a network or network devices. These IP addresses are configured as dotted decimal notation. An Internet Protocol (IP) address is a numerical identification and logical address that is assigned to devices participating in a computer network utilizing the Internet Protocol for communication between its nodes. Different classes of IP address are as follows:

- Class A networks consists of up to 16,777,214 client devices, and their address range can extend from 1 to 126.

- Class B networks consists of up to 65,534 client devices, and their address range can extend from 128 to 191.

- Class C networks consists of up to 245 client devices, and their address range can extend from 192 to 223.

- Class D networks addresses are reserved for multicasting, and their address range can extend from 224 to 239.

- Class E networks addresses are reserved for experimental purposes. Their addresses range from 240 to 254.

- Promiscuous mode or promisc mode is a configuration of a network card that makes the card pass all traffic it receives to the central processing unit rather than just packets addressed to it. This feature normally used for packet sniffing.

- Each packet includes the hardware (Media Access Control) address. When a network card receives a packet, it normally drops it unless the packet is addressed to that card. In promiscuous mode, however, the card allows all packets through, thus allowing the computer to read packets intended for other machines or network devices. Promiscuous mode is often used to diagnose network connectivity issues. It is also used by transparent network bridges in order to capture all traffic that needs to pass the bridge so that it can be retransmitted on the other side of the bridge.

- Failed Logon EventIDs are the range of security events that indicate logon failures. These event IDs are used to generate logged data with the help of SQL queries.

Event ID	Description
529	The logon attempt was made with an unknown username or a known username with a bad password.
530	The user account tried to log on outside the allowed time.
531	A logon attempt was made by using a disabled account.
532	A logon attempt was made by using an expired account.
533	The user is not allowed to log on at this computer.
534	The user attempted to log on with a logon type that is not allowed, such as network, interactive, batch, service, or remote interactive.
535	The password for the speci?ed account has expired.
537	The logon attempt failed for other reasons.
539	The account was locked out at the time the logon attempt was made. This event is logged when a user or

	computer attempts to authenticate with an account that has been previously locked out.

- Log parser is a command line utility that was written for use with the Windows operating system. The default behavior of log parser takes an SQL expression on the command line, outputs the lines containing matches for the SQL expression. The syntax of log parser is:

   $ logparser <options> <SQL expression>

- The Open systems Interconnection Model (OSI Model) is an abstract description for layered communications and computer network protocol design. It divides network architecture into seven layers which, from top to bottom, are the Application, Presentation, Session, Transport, Network, Data-Link, and Physical Layers.

- An IP address (Internet Protocol address) is a logical address that is used for providing a unique identity to a network or network devices.

- A sniffer is a software tool that is used to capture any network traffic. The Sniffer changes the NIC of the LAN card into promiscuous mode.

- Wireshark is a free packet sniffer computer application. It is used for network troubleshooting, analysis, software and communications protocol development, and education.

- Wireshark uses pcap to capture packets, so it can only capture the packets on the networks supported by pcap.

- Failed Logon EventIDs is the range of security events that indicate logon failures, and used to limit data to those specific events.

- IEEE 802.11b is an extension of the 802.11 standard. It is used in wireless local area networks (WLANs) and provides 11 Mbps transmission speeds in the bandwidth of 2.4 GHz.

- The access point works as a central bridge device to include wireless devices in the cabled LAN.

- Snort is an open source network intrusion prevention and detection system that operates as a network sniffer. It logs activities of the network that is matched with the predefined signatures. Signatures can be designed for a wide range of traffic, including Internet Protocol (IP), Transmission Control Protocol (TCP), User Datagram Protocol (UDP), and Internet Control Message Protocol (ICMP).

- A chain of custody is a documentation that shows who has collected and accessed each piece of evidence. It is a documentation of guidelines that computer forensics experts use to handle evidences.

Pop Quiz

Q1: At which OSI layer does UDP operate?

Ans: Transport layer

Q2: Sniffer operates at which layer of the OSI reference model?

Ans: Data link

- NetWitness is used to analyze and monitor the network traffic and activity.

- Netresident is used to capture, store, analyze, and reconstructs network events and activities.

Wireless Attacks

- Wireless Zero Configuration (WZC), also known as Wireless Auto Configuration, or WLAN AutoConfig is a wireless connection management utility included with Microsoft Windows XP and later operating systems as a service that dynamically selects a wireless network to connect to based on a user's preferences and various default settings. This can be used instead of, or in the absence of, a wireless network utility from the manufacturer of a computer's wireless networking device. The drivers for the wireless adapter query the NDIS Object IDs and pass the available network names to the service. WZC also introduce some security threats.

- WZC will probe for networks that are already connected. This information can be viewed by anyone using a wireless analyzer and can be used to set up fake access points to connect.

- WZC attempts to connect to the wireless network with the strongest signal. Attacker can create fake wireless networks with high-power antennas and cause computers to associate with his access point.

- 802.1X authentication, also known as WPA-Enterprise, is a security mechanism for wireless networks. 802.1X provides port-based authentication, which involves communications between a supplicant, authenticator, and authentication server. The supplicant is often software on a client device, the authenticator is a wired Ethernet switch or wireless access point, and an authentication server is generally a RADIUS database. The authenticator acts like a security guard to a protected network. The supplicant (client device) is not allowed access through the authenticator to the protected side of the network until the supplicant's identity is authorized. With 802.1X port-based authentication, the supplicant provides credentials, such as user name/password or digital certificate, to the authenticator, and the authenticator forwards the credentials to the authentication server for verification. If the credentials are valid, the supplicant (client device) is allowed to access resources located on the protected side of the network.

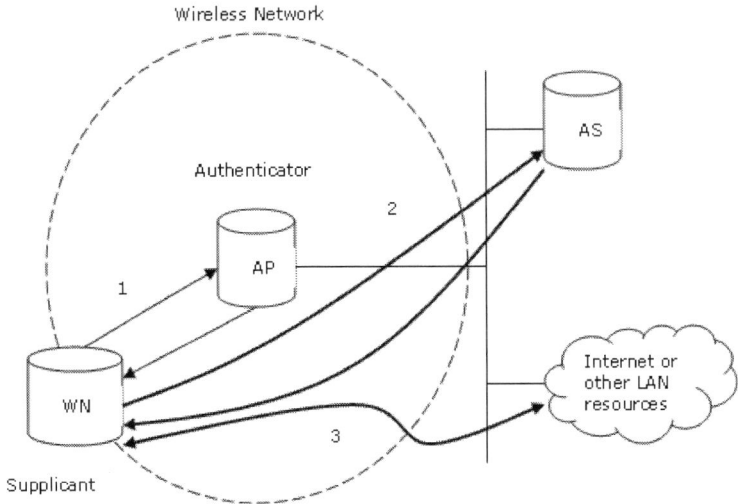

- An initialization vector (IV) is a block of bits that is required to allow a stream cipher or a block cipher to be executed in any of several streaming modes of operation to produce a unique stream independent from other streams produced by the same encryption key, without having to go through a re-keying process.

- The size of the IV depends on the encryption algorithm and on the cryptographic protocol in use and is normally as large as the block size of the cipher or as large as the encryption key. The IV must be known to the recipient of the encrypted information to be able to decrypt it.

- Ettercap is a Unix and Windows tool for computer network protocol analysis and security auditing. It is capable of intercepting traffic on a network segment, capturing passwords, and conducting active eavesdropping against a number of common protocols. It is a free open source software. Ettercap supports active and passive dissection of many protocols (including ciphered ones) and provides many features for network and host analysis.

- Nmap is a free open-source utility for network exploration and security auditing. It is used to discover computers and services on a computer network, thus creating a "map" of the network. Just like many simple port scanners, Nmap is capable of discovering passive services. In addition, Nmap may be able to determine various details about the remote computers. These include operating system, device type, uptime, software product used to run a service, exact version number of that product, presence of some firewall techniques and, on a local area network, even vendor of the remote network card. Nmap runs on Linux, Microsoft Windows etc.

- The general format for writing MAC addresses is to use six group of two hexadecimal digits, each separated by hyphen.

- Microsoft provides the Windows Wireless Zero Configuration (WZC) utility to assist the user with connecting to wireless networks. It makes the association process easier.

- IEEE 802.1X is an IEEE Standard for port-based Network Access Control. 802.1X authentication is a security mechanism for wireless networks. 802.1X provides port-based authentication, which involves communications between a supplicant, authenticator, and authentication server.

- Nmap is a free open-source utility for network exploration and security auditing. It is used to discover computers and services on a computer network, thus creating a "map" of the network.

- WEP uses the RC4 encryption algorithm. The main drawback of WEP is that its Initialization Vector (IV) field is only 24 bits long.

- SSIDs are case sensitive text strings and have a maximum length of 32 characters.

- Wired Equivalent Privacy (WEP) is a security protocol for Wireless Local Area Networks (WLANs). It has two components, authentication and encryption. It provides security, which is equivalent to wired networks, for wireless networks.WPA stands for Wi-Fi Protected Access.

It is a wireless security standard. It provides better security than WEP (Wired Equivalent Protection).

- WEP supports three encryption modes, i.e., no encryption, 40 bit encryption, and 128 bit encryption.

- Only users with the correct WEP key can authenticate from the access point of the network.

- SSL uses a combination of public key and symmetric encryption to provide communication privacy, authentication, and message integrity for secure browsing on the Internet.

- Wireless Local Area Network (WLAN) is a network that enables devices to connect to the network wirelessly. WLAN uses radiated energy, commonly called high-frequency radio waves, to communicate amongst nodes.

- ITU-R (International Telecommunications Union-Radio communication) is a worldwide organization of United Nations. It works for standardization of communications that use radiated energy. Its prime objective is to manage the assignment of frequencies.

- IEEE (Institute of Electrical and Electronic Engineers) is a society of technical professionals. It promotes the development and application of electro-technology and allied sciences. IEEE develops communications and network standards, among other activities. The organization publishes a number of journals, have many local chapters, and societies in specialized areas.

- Wi-Fi Alliance is an industry consortium that encourages interoperability of products that use WLAN standards. The consortium runs a certification program and recognizes products, which are implementing WLAN standards, as Wi-Fi certified products.

- FCC (Federal Communications Commission) is an independent US government agency. It regulates interstate and international communications by radio, television, wire, satellite and cable in the United States of America.

- An ad hoc network consists of two or more wireless devices that communicate directly with each other. The wireless local area network (WLAN) network interface adapters in the wireless devices generate omni directional signals within a limited range called Basic Service Area (BSA). When two wireless devices come within the range of each other, they immediately form a two-node network and are able to communicate with each other.

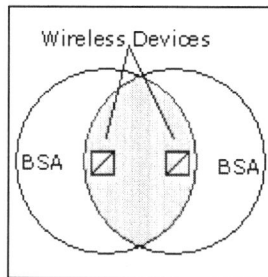

- An infrastructure network consists of an access point that connects wireless devices to the standard cable network. An access point is connected to cabled network through a cable and it generates omni directional signals. When wireless devices come within the range of the access point, they are able to communicate with the cabled local area network.

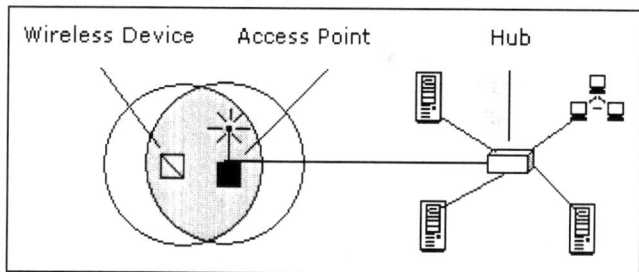

- An ad hoc network is non-transitive.

- 802.11 is the latest networking specification for wireless local area networks (WLANs), developed by the Institute of Electrical and Electronic Engineers. It contains several sub-specifications , and the IEEE is constantly adding new specifications. This specification uses Carrier Sense

Multiple Access with Collision Avoidance (CSMS/CA) media access control mechanism. 802.11 supports 1 or 2 Mbps transmission in the 2.4 GHz ISM band using Frequency Hopping Spread Spectrum (FHSS).

- 802.11x contains various specifications for the 802.11 family of Wireless LAN network standards. Some of the specifications in this family are still under development. The 802.11b specification uses Direct Sequence Spread Spectrum (DSSS) and supports 11 Mbps transmission in the 2.4 GHz band.

Pop Quiz

Q1: On which of the following encryption algorithms, WEP is based?

Ans: RC4

Q2: Which of the following tools is a wireless sniffer and analyzer that works on the Windows operating system?

Ans: Aeropeek

- Infrared technology uses invisible infrared radiations to transmit signals to short distances. There are two types of networks communication possible, one in which the sender and the receiver are visible to each other and are situated in a straight line known as line-of-sight mode; the other type of communication known as diffuse mode does not require the sender and receiver to be directly visible to each other. This technology is used in TV sets, cordless microphones, laptops, remote modems, printers, and other peripheral devices. Infrared networks use frequencies in the terahertz range and support transmission speeds of 1 to 2 Mbps.

- Bluetooth technology uses short-range radio frequencies to transmit voice and data signals at the speed of 1 Mbps on a frequency of 2.4 Ghz. Bluetooth is used to automatically synchronize information among different types of computers like desktops, laptops, and palmtops, or connecting to the Internet through a cell phone.

- Wireless Application Protocol (WAP) supports mobile computing. It was developed by the WAP forum. The functionality of WAP is equivalent to that of TCP/IP. WAP uses a smaller version of HTML called Wireless Markup Language (WML) to display Internet sites.

- Wired Equivalent Privacy (WEP) is a security protocol for wireless local area networks (WLANs). It has two components, authentication and encryption. It provides security, which is equivalent to wired networks, for wireless networks. WEP encrypts data on a wireless network by using a fixed secret key. WEP incorporates a checksum in each frame to provide protection against the attacks that attempt to reveal the key stream.

- The Institute of Electrical and Electronics Engineering (IEEE) is a leading organization in the world. It constituted a task force to set standards for connectivity between NIC and transmission media. This task force is known as the 802 committee. The 802 committee was subdivided into several sub groups and each group is responsible for the implementation of a single standard that specifies the data transfer that occurs at the data link layer of the OSI model.

Types of Web Attacks, Different Tools for locating IP address

- Hacking process consists of a fixed approach or methodology. Hacking refers to the act of penetrating or gaining unauthorized access to computer systems for creating or modifying computer software and hardware, including computer programming, administration, and security-related items. A Hacker is a person who breaks into computers, usually by gaining access of administrative level. Hackers use various methods to accomplish the task. These methods are sequentially followed by a malicious hacker to accomplish his objective. These methods are widely divided in the following six phases:

  1. Reconnaissance

  2. Scanning

3. Gaining access

4. Escalation of privilege

5. Maintaining access

6. Covering tracks

- Cross-site request forgery, also known as one-click attack or session riding, is a type of malicious exploit of a website whereby unauthorized commands are transmitted from a user that the website trusts. Unlike cross-site scripting (XSS), which exploits the trust a user has for a particular site, CSRF exploits the trust that a site has in a user's browser. The attack works by including a link or script in a page that accesses a site to which the user is known to have authenticated.

- A code injection attack exists whenever a scripting or programming language is used in a Web page. All that the attacker needs is an error or opening. That opening usually comes in the form of an input field that is not validated correctly. It is not necessary for the code injection attack to be on the Web page. It can be located in the back end as part of a database query of the Web site. If any part of the server uses Java, JavaScript, C, SQL, or any other code between the Internet and the data, it is vulnerable to the code injection attack.

- A command injection attack is used to inject and execute commands specified by the attacker in the vulnerable application. The application, which executes unwanted system commands, is like a virtual system shell. The attacker may use it as any authorized system user. However, commands are executed with the same privileges and environment as the application has. The command injection attacks are possible in most cases because of lack of correct input data validation, which can be manipulated by the attacker.

- A demilitarized zone (DMZ) is a physical or logical subnetwork that contains and exposes external services of an organization to a larger network, usually the Internet. The purpose of a DMZ is to add an additional layer of security to an organization's Local Area Network (LAN); an external attacker only has access to equipment in the DMZ, rather than the whole of the network. Hosts in the DMZ have limited connectivity to specific hosts in the internal network, though communication with other hosts in the DMZ and to the external network is allowed. This allows hosts in the DMZ to provide services to both the internal and external networks, while an intervening firewall controls the traffic between the DMZ servers and the internal network clients. In a DMZ configuration, most computers on the LAN run behind a firewall connected to a public network such as the Internet.

- A zero-day attack or threat is a computer threat that tries to exploit computer application vulnerabilities that are unknown to others, undisclosed to the software vendor, or for which no security fix is available. Zero-day exploits are used or shared by attackers before the software vendor knows about the vulnerability.

- The hacking process follows a fixed methodology. The steps a hacker follows can be broadly divided into six phases.

- Cross-site scripting (XSS) is a type of computer security vulnerability typically found in Web applications, which allow code injection by malicious Web users into the Web pages viewed by other users.

- Cross-site scripting (XSS) is a type of computer security vulnerability typically found in Web applications, which allow code injection by malicious Web users into the Web pages viewed by other users. Various methods are used to investigate Cross-Site Scripting attack.

- A code injection attack exists whenever a scripting or programming language is used in a Web page.

- A demilitarized zone (DMZ) is a physical or logical subnetwork that contains and exposes external services of an organization to a larger network, usually the Internet. An external attacker only has access to equipment in the DMZ, rather than the whole of the network.

- Hypertext Transfer Protocol Secure (HTTPS) protocol is a protocol used in the Universal Resource Locater (URL) address line to connect to a secure site.

- Persistent type of Cross-Site Scripting (XSS) exists when data provided to a Web application by a user is first stored persistently on the server (in a database, or other location), and later displayed to users in a Web page without being encoded using HTML entities. Example of this is with online message boards or Internet forums, where users are allowed to post HTML formatted messages for other users to read.

- Non-persistent type of Cross-Site Scripting (XSS) occurs when data provided by a Web client is used immediately by server-side scripts to generate a page of results for that user. If unvalidated user-supplied data are included in the resulting page without HTML encoding, this will allow client-side code to be injected into the dynamic page. One of the most common example for this is a search engine.

- DOM based Cross-Site Scripting attack, the problem exists within the pages of client-side script. If a piece of JavaScript accesses a URL request parameter and uses this information to write some HTML to its own page. However, this information is not encoded using HTML entities; Cross-Site Scripting (XSS) hole will likely be present. This written data will be re-interpreted by browsers as HTML, which could include additional client-side scripts.

Pop Quiz

Q1: Which protocol does Microsoft Windows use for traceroute?

Ans: ICMP

Q2: Which of the following tools is an open source network intrusion prevention and detection system that operates as a network sniffer?

Ans: Snort

- SAX is a parsing mechanism for XML.

Hacking Routers and Router Attack topology

- A router is a purposely customized computer used to forward data among computer networks beyond directly connected devices.

- More technically, a router is a networking device whose software and hardware are customized to the tasks of routing and forwarding information. A router differs from an ordinary computer in that it needs special hardware, called interface cards, to connect to remote devices through either copper cables or Optical fiber cable. These interface cards are in fact small computers that are specialized to convert electric signals from one form to another, with embedded CPU or ASIC, or both. In the case of optical fiber, the interface cards (also called ports) convert between optical signals and electrical signals.

- Hopcount is a measure of distance across an IP-based network. It is a count of the number of routers an IP packet has to pass through in order to reach its destination. Hopcount is usually not used by itself, since any in between router or cable may have or be subject to varying data bandwidth, load, reliability (especially of cable), and latency. Hopcounts are often useful to find faults in a network, or to discover if routing is indeed correct.

- A Sequence++ attack creates an unstable network. It could contribute to a DoS condition. The hacker continually injects a larger LSA sequence number, which indicates to the network that it has a fresher route. The original router corrects this LSA sequence number in the process known as "fight back" by sending its own LSA with a newer sequence number than the hackers sequence number.

- The Max Age attack causes network confusion. It may contribute to a DoS condition. The maximum age of a LSA is 3600 seconds (one hour). Hacker sends LSA packets with maxage set. The original router that sent this LSA then corrects the sudden change in age by generating a refresh message. This process is known as "fight-back". Hacker continually interjects packets with the maxage value for a given routing value, which causes network instability.

- Route table poisoning is a method of quickly removing outdated routing information from other router's routing tables by changing its hop count to be unreachable (higher than the maximum number of hops allowed) and sending a routing update. When a router receives a route poisoning, it sends an update back to the router from which it received the route poisoning, this is called poison reverse. This is to ensure that all routers on a segment have received the poisoned route information.

- Routers are hardware or software devices that are used to route data from a local area network to a different network.

- The router table is maintained by routers to determine the interface to which an incoming packet has to be forwarded. The routing table consists of several parameters on the basis of which the best path is determined.

- The hop count is a measure of distance across an IP-based network. It is a count of the number of routers an IP packet has to pass through in order to reach its destination.

- Many attackers target routers, and launch attacks against them. These attacks may focus on configuration errors, known vulnerabilities, or even weak passwords.

- Hypertext Transfer Protocol Secure (HTTPS) protocol is a protocol used in the Universal Resource Locater (URL) address line to connect to a secure site.

Pop Quiz

Q1: Routers work at which layer of the OSI reference model?

Ans: Network

Q2: Which of the following distributes incorrect IP address to divert the traffic?

Ans: DNS poisioning

Test Your Knowledge

Q1. Which of the following standards is used in wireless local area networks (WLANs)?

A.   IEEE 802.3

B.   IEEE 802.11b

C.   IEEE 802.4

D.   IEEE 802.5

Q2. You work as a Network Administrator for NetTech Inc. The company has a network that consists of 200 client computers and ten database servers. One morning, you find that a hacker is accessing unauthorized data on a database server on the network. Which of the following actions will you take to preserve the evidences?

Each correct answer represents a complete solution. Choose three.

A.   Prevent a forensics experts team from entering the server room.

B.   Prevent the company employees from entering the server room.

C.   Preserve the log files for a forensics expert.

D.   Detach the network cable from the database server.

Q3. Which of the following is a documentation of guidelines that computer forensics experts use to handle evidences?

A.   Chain of evidence

B.   Evidence access policy

C.   Chain of custody

D.   Incident response policy

Q4. You work as a Network Administrator for Tech Perfect Inc. The company has a Windows Active Directory-based single domain single forest network. The functional level of the forest is Windows Server 2003. The company has recently provided fifty laptops to its sales team members. You are required to configure an 802.11 wireless network for the laptops. The sales team members must be able to use their data placed at a server in a cabled network. The planned network should be able to handle the threat of unauthorized access and data interception by an unauthorized user. You are also required to prevent the sales team members from communicating directly to one another. Which of the following actions will you take to accomplish the task?

Each correct answer represents a complete solution. Choose all that apply.

A.   Using group policies, configure the network to allow the wireless computers to connect to the infrastructure networks only.

B.   Implement the open system authentication for the wireless network.

C.   Implement the IEEE 802.1X authentication for the wireless network.

D.   Using group policies, configure the network to allow the wireless computers to connect to the ad hoc networks only.

E.   Configure the wireless network to use WEP encryption for the data transmitted over a wireless network.

Q5. Every network device contains a unique built in Media Access Control (MAC) address, which is used to identify the authentic device to limit the network access. Which of the following addresses is a valid MAC address?

A.   1011-0011-1010-1110-1100-0001

B.   A3-07-B9-E3-BC-F9

C.   132.298.1.23

D.   F936.28A1.5BCD.DEFA

Answer Explanation

A1.   Answer option B is correct.

IEEE 802.11b is an extension of the 802.11 standard. It is used in wireless local area networks (WLANs) and provides 11 Mbps transmission speeds in the bandwidth of 2.4 GHz.

Answer option A is incorrect. IEEE 802.3 is a standard for wired networks , which defines the media access control (MAC) layer for bus networks that use CSMA/CD.

Answer option C is incorrect. IEEE 802.4 is a standard for wired networks , which defines the MAC layer for bus networks that use a token-passing mechanism.

Answer option D is incorrect. IEEE 802.5 is a standard for wired networks, which defines the MAC layer for token-ring networks.

A2.   Answer options B, C, and D are correct.

To preserve the evidences, You will take the following steps:

Prevent the company employees from entering the server room.

Preserve the log files for a forensics expert for further investigation.

Detach the network cable from the database server to prevent the user from accessing further data.

A3.   Answer option C is correct.

A chain of custody is a documentation that shows who has collected and accessed each piece of evidence. The documentation must be meticulously prepared including the minutest details (such as the date, time, location, and the verified identity of every person handling the evidence) so that the documentation is verifiable. It includes the time of accessing the evidence and the valid reason for doing so. A chain of custody must be maintained for all evidences in order to maintain the validity of the evidences.

Answer option D is incorrect. Incident response policy is a document that defines an incident and helps people to respond appropriately to that incident. It provides information about people who are responsible for handling security incidents and how they can be contacted. The incident response policy also provides instructions to deal with documenting and disseminating incident-related information.

A4.   Answer options A, C, and E are correct.

In order to enable wireless networking, you have to install access points in various areas of your office building. These access points generate omni directional signals to broadcast network traffic. Unauthorized users can intercept these packets. Hence, security is the major concern for a wireless network. The two primary threats are unauthorized access and data interception. In order to accomplish the task, you will have to take the following steps:

• Using group policies, configure the network to allow the wireless computers to connect to the infrastructure networks only. This will prevent the sales team members from communicating directly to one another.

• Implement the IEEE 802.1X authentication for the wireless network. This will allow only authenticated users to access the network data and resources.

• Configure the wireless network to use WEP encryption for data transmitted over a wireless network. This will encrypt the network data packets transmitted over wireless connections. Although WEP encryption does not prevent intruders from capturing the packets, it prevents them from reading the data inside.

Answer option B is incorrect. Open System authentication is the default authentication method used by 802.11 devices. But, in fact, it provides no authentication at all. It exchanges messages between the two wireless devices without using any password or keys. A device configured to use the Open System authentication cannot refuse to authenticate another device.

Answer option D is incorrect. The ad hoc networks enable users to communicate directly to one another, whereas the question clearly states that you should prevent the sales team members from communicating directly to one another.

A5. Answer option B is correct.

The general format for writing MAC addresses is to use six group of two hexadecimal digits, each separated by hyphen (-). Another standard method is also used for writing MAC addresses as three groups of four hexadecimal digits separated by dots.

Answer option A is incorrect. Binary numbers are not used to denote MAC address.

Answer option C is incorrect. This is an example of IP address.

Answer option D is incorrect. This is not a valid MAC address as there four groups of four hexadecimal digits exist.

Chapter 8 - Investigating DOS attacks and Internet crimes, Tracking E-Mail.

Overview

A Denial-of-Service (DoS) attack is mounted with the objective of causing a negative impact on the performance of a computer or network. It is also known as network saturation attack or bandwidth consumption attack. Attackers make Denial-of-Service attacks by sending a large number of protocol packets to a network. A DoS attack can cause the following to occur:

- o   Saturate network resources.
- o   Disrupt connections between two computers, thereby preventing communications between services.
- o   Disrupt services to a specific computer. A computer network, often simply referred to as a network, is a collection of computers and devices connected by communications channels that facilitates communications among users and allows users to share resources with other users. Networks may be classified according to a wide variety of characteristics.

Key Points

Types of DOS Attacks.

- • A SYN Attack is a common denial-of-service (DoS) technique. Using this technique, an attacker sends multiple SYN packets to the target computer. For each SYN packet received, the target computer allocates resources and sends an acknowledgement (SYN-ACK) to the source IP address. Since the target computer does not receive a response from the attacking computer, it attempts to resend the SYN-ACK. This leaves TCP ports in a half-open state. When an attacker sends TCP SYNs repeatedly, the target computer eventually runs out of resources and is unable to handle any more connections, thereby denying services to legitimate users.

- In the smurf DoS attack, an attacker sends a large amount of ICMP echo requests traffic to the IP broadcast addresses. These ICMP requests have a spoofed source address of the intended victim. If the routing device delivering traffic to those broadcast addresses delivers the IP broadcast to all hosts, most of the IP addresses send ECHO reply message. On a multi-access broadcast network, hundreds of computers might reply to each packet. Now the target network is overwhelmed by all the messages sent simultaneously, so the network becomes unable to provide services to all the messages and gets crashed.

- In the ping of death attack, the attacker sends ICMP packet larger than 65,536 bytes. Since the operating system does not know how to handle the packet size larger than 65,536 bytes, either the operating system freezes or crashes at the time of reassembling of the packet. But, nowadays the operating systems discard such packets, so ping of death attack is not applicable at the present time.

- In the jolt DoS attack, an attacker fragments the ICMP packet in such a manner that the target computer cannot reassemble it. In this situation, the CPU utilization of the target system becomes 100 percent and the system gets crashed.

- In the land attack, the attacker sends the spoofed TCP SYN packet in which the IP address of the target is filled in both source and destination fields. Now, on receiving the spoofed packet the target system becomes confused and goes into the frozen state. Nowadays the antivirus can easily detect such attacks.

- In the ping flood attack, the attacker sends large number of ICMP packets to the target computer using the ping command, i.e., ping -f target_IP_address. Now when the target computer receives ICMP packets in a large quantity, it does not respond and gets hanged. However, for such attacks, the attacker must have greater Internet bandwidth, because if the target responds ECHO reply

ICMP packet, the attacker must have both the incoming and outgoing bandwidths available for communication.

- In the fraggle DoS attack, the attacker sends a large number of UDP echo requests traffic to IP broadcast addresses. These UDP requests have a spoofed source address of the intended victim. If the routing device delivering traffic to those broadcast addresses delivers the IP broadcast to all hosts, most of the IP addresses send ECHO reply message; on a multi-access broadcast network, hundreds of machines might reply to each packet. Now the target network is overwhelmed by all the messages sent simultaneously, so it becomes unable to provide service to all the messages and gets crashed.

- The TCP FTP proxy (bounce attack) scanner connects to an FTP server and requests that server to start data transfer to the third system. Now, the scanner uses the PORT FTP command to declare whether or not the data transfer process is listening at the certain port number. Then the scanner uses LIST FTP command to list the current directory. This result is sent over the server. If the data transfer is successful, it is clear that the port is open. If the port is closed, the attacker receives the connection refused ICMP error message.

- In the teardrop attack, a series of data packets are sent to the target computer with overlapping offset field values. As a result, the target computer is unable to reassemble such packets and forced to crash, hang, or reboot.

- Address Resolution Protocol (ARP) spoofing, also known as ARP poisoning or ARP Poison Routing (APR), is a technique used to attack an Ethernet wired or wireless network. ARP spoofing may allow an attacker to sniff data frames on a local area network (LAN), modify the traffic, or stop the traffic altogether. The attack can only be used on networks that actually make use of ARP and not another method of address resolution. The principle of ARP spoofing is to send fake ARP messages to an Ethernet LAN. Generally, the aim is to associate the attacker's MAC address with the IP address of another node (such as the default gateway). Any traffic meant for that IP address would be mistakenly sent to the attacker instead. The attacker could then choose to forward the traffic to the actual default gateway (passive sniffing) or modify the data before forwarding it. ARP spoofing attacks can be run from a compromised host, or from an attacker's machine that is connected directly to the target Ethernet segment.

- The fork bomb is a form of denial-of-service attack against a computer system. A fork bomb works by creating a large number of processes very quickly in order to saturate the available space in the list of processes kept by the operating system of computers. If the process table becomes saturated, no new programs may start until another process terminates. Even if that happens, it is not likely that a useful program may be started since the instances of the bomb program will each attempt to take any newly-available slot themselves. Fork bombs count as wabbits: they typically do not spread as worms or viruses. To incapacitate a system, they rely on the assumption that the number of programs and processes that may execute simultaneously on a computer has a limit.

- In a ping of death attack, the attacker sends an ICMP packet larger than 65,536 bytes. Since the operating system does not know how to handle a packet larger than 65,536 bytes, it either freezes or crashes at the time of reassembling the packet.

- In a fraggle DoS attack, an attacker sends a UDP echo request message, whereas in a smurf DoS attack, an attacker sends an ICMP echo request message.

- TFN, Trin00, Stacheldraht, Saft, and Mstream are some good DDoS attack tools.

- A Denial-of-Service attack (DoS attack) is an attempt to make a computer resource unavailable to its intended users. DoS attacks are implemented by either forcing the targeted computers to reset, or consuming its resources so that it can no longer provide its intended service.

- A Denial-of-Service (DoS) attack is performed by sending a large number of protocol packets to the network.

- In a Distributed Denial of Service (DDoS) attack, an attacker uses multiple computers throughout the network that it has previously infected. Such computers act as zombies and work together to send out bogus messages, thereby increasing the amount of traffic.

- A Denial-of-Service (DoS) attack is mounted with the objective of causing a negative impact on the performance of a computer or a network. DoS attacks are performed by sending a large number of protocol packets to the network.

Pop Quiz

Q1: Which DoS attack is a multi-tier attack?

Ans: DDoS Attack

Q2: Which DoS attack points the Central Processing Unit (CPU) to a non-existent memory location causing the running process to end abruptly?

Ans: Buffer Overflow Attack

- The network-ingress filtering can be used as prevention from DDoS attacks.

- The countermeasures against a smurf DoS attack are to disable IP-directed broadcasts and to configure local computers so as not to respond to such ICMP packets that are configured to be sent to IP broadcast addresses.

Cyber Crimes and Internet Tools

- A buffer-overflow attack is performed when a hacker fills a field, typically an address bar, with more characters than it can accommodate. The excess characters can be run as executable code, effectively giving the hacker control of the computer and overriding any security measures set. There are two main types of buffer overflow attacks:

    i. Stack-based buffer overflow attack uses a memory object known as a stack. The hacker develops the code which reserves a specific amount of space for the stack. If the input of user is longer than the amount of space reserved for it within the stack, then the stack will overflow.

ii. Heap-based overflow attack floods the memory space reserved for the programs.

- The Federal Trade Commission (FTC) is an independent agency of the United States government, established in 1914 by the Federal Trade Commission Act. Its principal mission is the promotion of "consumer protection" and the elimination and prevention of what regulators perceive to be harmfully "anti-competitive" business practices, such as coercive monopoly. FTC has been delegated the enforcement of additional business regulation statutes and has promulgated a number of regulations.

- By executing buffer overflow attack, hacker can read the working storage area of memory and the unencrypted cookie data. Evidence of Buffer Overflow or Cookie Snooping attack can be retrieved from system logs, event logs, and program logs.

- A user can hide his identity using a firewall, proxy server, or anonymizer.

- Spam or unsolicited commercial e-mail is both annoying and wastes time, resulting in economic loss. Various steps can be taken to stop the Spam.

- A proxy server hides the identity of a user's system from the outside world. Instead of creating connection directly with the remote host, the user's system creates a direct connection with the proxy server, and the proxy server establishes a connection with the remote host to which the user wants to connect.

- Anonymizers are the services that help make a user's own Web surfing anonymous. An anonymizer removes all the identifying information from a user's computer while the user surfs the Internet. In this manner, it ensures the privacy of the user. After the user anonymizes a Web access with an anonymizer prefix, every subsequent link selected is also automatically accessed anonymously. Most anonymizers can anonymize at least the Web (http:), file transfer protocol (ftp:), and gopher (gopher:) Internet services.

- IPChains is a linux packet filtering firewall that allows a Network Administrator to ACCEPT, DENY, MASQ, or REDIRECT packets.

- A rootkit is a set of tools that take Administrative control of a computer system without authorization by the computer owners and/or legitimate managers. A rootkit requires root access to be installed in the Linux operating system, but once installed, the attacker can get root access at any time.

Pop Quiz

Q1: Which of the following encryption techniques does digital signatures use?

Ans:MD5

Q2: Which TCP/UDP port is used by the toolkit program netstat?

Ans: Port 15

E-Mail sending-receiving System

- An e-mail storm is a sudden spike of Reply All messages on an e-mail distribution list, usually caused by a controversial or misdirected message. Such storms start when multiple members of the distribution list reply to the entire list at the same time in response to an instigating message. Other members soon respond, usually adding vitriol to the discussion, asking to be removed from the list, or pleading for the cessation of messages. If enough members reply to these unwanted messages, this triggers a chain reaction of e-mail messages. The sheer load of traffic generated by these storms can render the e-mail servers carrying them inoperative, similar to a DDoS attack. Some e-mail viruses also have the capacity to create e-mail storms, by sending copies of themselves to an infected user's contacts, including distribution lists, infecting the contacts in turn.

- E-mail spoofing is a term used to describe e-mail activity in which the sender address and other parts of the e-mail header are altered to appear as though the e-mail originated from a different source. E-mail spoofing is a technique commonly used for spam e-mail and phishing to hide the origin of an e-mail message. By changing certain properties of the e-mail, such as the From, Return-Path, and Reply-To fields (which can be found in the message header), ill-intentioned users can make the e-mail appear to be from someone other than the actual sender. The result is that, although the e-mail appears to come from the address indicated in the From field, it actually comes from another source.

- Syslog is a standard for forwarding log messages in an IP network. The term "Syslog" is often used for both the actual Syslog protocol, as well as the application or library sending Syslog messages. Syslog is a client/server protocol. The Syslog sender sends a small textual message to the Syslog receiver. The receiver is commonly called Syslogd. Syslog messages can be sent via UDP or TCP. Syslog is typically used for computer system management and security auditing. While it has a number of shortcomings, Syslog is supported by a wide variety of devices and receivers across multiple platforms. Because of this, Syslog can be used to integrate log data from many different types of systems into a central repository.

- The email header holds information about the origin of the email. This will include the IP address of the source, the method used to send it, and who is the sender. Each message has exactly one header, which is structured into fields. Each field has a name and a value. The field name starts in the first character of the line and ends before the separator character ":". The separator is then followed by the field value. Field names and values are restricted to 7-bit ASCII characters. Non-ASCII values may be represented using MIME encoded words.

- Messaging Application Programming Interface (MAPI) is a messaging architecture and a Component Object Model based API for Microsoft Windows. MAPI allows client programs to become (e-mail) messaging-enabled, -aware, or -based by calling MAPI subsystem routines that interface with certain messaging servers. While MAPI is designed to be independent of the protocol, it is usually used with MAPI/RPC, the proprietary protocol that Microsoft Outlook uses to communicate with Microsoft Exchange. Simple MAPI is a subset of 12 functions which enable developers to add basic messaging functionality. Extended MAPI allows complete control over the messaging system on the client computer, creation and management of messages, management of the client mailbox, service providers, and so forth.

- Extensible Storage Engine (ESE), also known as JET Blue, is an Indexed Sequential Access Method (ISAM) data storage technology from Microsoft. ESE is notably a core of Microsoft Exchange Server and Active Directory. Its purpose is to allow applications to store and retrieve data via indexed and sequential access. Windows Mail and Desktop Search in the Windows Vista operating system also make use of ESE to store indexes and property information respectively. ESE provides transacted data update and retrieval. A crash recovery mechanism is provided so that data consistency is maintained even in the event of a system crash. Transactions in ESE are highly concurrent, making ESE suitable for server applications. ESE caches data intelligently to ensure high performance access to data. In addition, ESE is lightweight, making it suitable for auxiliary applications.

- Spam is a term that refers to the unsolicited e-mails sent to a large number of e-mail users.

- An e-mail message is composed of a message header and the subject body. The e-mail header is important because it holds information about the origin of the email. This includes the IP address of the source, the method used to send it, who sent it, etc.

- Microsoft Outlook allows the user to save e-mail messages in two different file formats based on the system configuration.

- Online e-mail systems such as Hotmail and Yahoo leave files containing e-mail message information on the local computer. These files are stored in a number of folders.

- /var/log/mailog file generally contains the source and destination IP addresses, date and time stamps, and other information that may be used to validate the information contained within an e-mail header.

- The EDB database files, STM database files, checkpoint files, and the temporary files are the main concern of a professional Computer Hacking Forensic Investigator while investigating emails that are sent using a Microsoft Exchange.

- An open relay is the most common method for an attacker to spoof email.

- Malicious e-mails can be prevented from entering the network from the non-existing domains by enabling DNS reverse lookup on the e-mail server. DNS reverse lookup enhances the security of a network by confirming the identity of incoming e-mails.

Test Your Knowledge

Q1. In which of the following DoS attacks does an attacker send an ICMP packet larger than 65,536 bytes to the target system?

A.   Jolt

B.   Ping of death

C.   Teardrop

D.   Fraggle

Q2. Maria works as a professional Ethical Hacker. She is assigned a project to test the security of www.we-are-secure.com. She wants to test a DoS attack on the We-are-secure server. She finds that the firewall of the server is blocking the ICMP messages, but it is not checking the UDP packets. Therefore, she sends a large amount of UDP echo request traffic to the IP broadcast addresses. These UDP requests have a spoofed source address of the We-are-secure server. Which of the following DoS attacks is Maria using to accomplish her task?

A.   Fraggle DoS attack

B.   Smurf DoS attack

C.   Ping flood attack

D.   Teardrop attack

Q3. John works as a professional Ethical Hacker. He is assigned a project to test the security of www.we-are-secure.com. He wants to test the response of a DDoS attack on the we-are-secure server. To accomplish this, he takes the following steps:

- Instead of directly attacking the target computer, he first identifies a less secure network named Infosecure that contains a network of 100 computers.

- He breaks this less secure network and takes control of all its computers. After completing this step, he installs a DDoS attack tool on each computer of the Infosecure network.

- Finally, he uses all the computers of the less secure network to carry out the DDoS attack on the we-are-secure server.

Which of the following tools can John use to accomplish the task?

Each correct answer represents a complete solution. Choose all that apply.

A. TFN

B. Trin00

C. Stacheldraht

D. BackOfficer Friendly

Q4. Which of the following Denial-of-Service (DoS) attacks employ IP fragmentation mechanism?

Each correct answer represents a complete solution. Choose two.

A. Teardrop attack

B. SYN flood attack

C. Ping of Death attack

D. Land attack

Q5. In which of the following DoS attacks does an attacker send an ICMP packet larger than 65,536 bytes to the target system?

A. Jolt

B. Ping of death

C. Teardrop

D. Fraggle

Answer Explanation

A1. Answer option B is correct.

In a ping of death attack, the attacker sends an ICMP packet larger than 65,536 bytes. Since the operating system does not know how to handle a packet larger than 65,536 bytes, it either freezes or crashes at the time of reassembling the packet. However, nowadays the operating systems discard such packets, so the ping of death attack is not applicable under these circumstances.

Answer option A is incorrect. In the jolt DoS attack, an attacker fragments the ICMP packet in such a manner that the target computer cannot reassemble it. In this situation, the CPU utilization of the target system becomes 100 percent and the system gets crashed.

Answer option C is incorrect. In a teardrop attack, a series of data packets are sent to the target computer with overlapping offset field values. As a result, the target computer is unable to reassemble these packets and is forced to crash, hang, or reboot.

Answer option D is incorrect. In a fraggle DoS attack, an attacker sends a large amount of UDP echo request traffic to the IP broadcast addresses. These UDP requests have a spoofed source address of the intended victim. If the routing device delivering traffic to those broadcast addresses delivers the IP broadcast to all the hosts, most of the IP addresses send an ECHO reply message. However, on a multi-access broadcast network, hundreds of computers might reply to each packet when the target network is overwhelmed by all the messages sent simultaneously. Due to this, the network becomes unable to provide services to all the messages and crashes.

A2. Answer option A is correct.

In the given scenario, Maria is using a fraggle DoS attack to accomplish her task. In a fraggle DoS attack, an attacker sends a large amount of UDP echo request traffic to the IP broadcast addresses. These UDP requests have a spoofed source address of the intended victim. If the routing device delivering traffic to those broadcast addresses delivers the IP broadcast to all the hosts, most of the IP addresses send an ECHO reply message. However, on a multi-access broadcast network, hundreds of computers might reply to each packet when the target network is overwhelmed by all the messages sent simultaneously. Due to this, the network becomes unable to provide services to all the messages and crashes.

Answer option B is incorrect. In a smurf DoS attack, an attacker sends a large amount of ICMP echo request traffic to the IP broadcast addresses. These ICMP requests have a spoofed source address of the intended victim. If the routing device delivering traffic to those broadcast addresses delivers the IP broadcast to all the hosts, most of the IP addresses send an ECHO reply message. However, on a multi-access broadcast network, hundreds of computers might reply to each packet when the target network is overwhelmed by all the messages sent simultaneously. Due to this, the network becomes unable to provide services to all the messages and crashes.

Answer option C is incorrect. In a ping flood attack, an attacker sends a large number of ICMP packets to the target computer using the ping command, i.e., ping -f target_IP_address. When the target computer receives these packets in large quantities, it does not respond and hangs. However, for such an attack to take place, the attacker must have sufficient Internet bandwidth, because if the target responds with an "ECHO reply ICMP packet" message, the attacker must have both the incoming and outgoing bandwidths available for communication.

Answer option D is incorrect. In a teardrop attack, a series of data packets are sent to the target computer with overlapping offset field values. As a result, the target computer is unable to reassemble these packets and is forced to crash, hang, or reboot.

A3. Answer options A, B, and C are correct.

TFN, Trin00, Stacheldraht, Saft, and Mstream are some good DDoS attack tools. Therefore, John can use any of these tools to accomplish his task.

Answer option D is incorrect. John will not use BackOfficer Friendly because it is an open source Honeypot, which is used to lure an attacker from a critical system.

A4. Answer options A and C are correct.

The Teardrop attack and the Ping of Death attack employ IP fragmentation mechanism.

A Teardrop attack involves sending mangled IP fragments with overlapping, over-sized, payloads to the target machine. This can crash various operating systems due to a bug in their TCP/IP fragmentation re-assembly code. In a teardrop attack, a series of data packets are sent to the target computer with overlapping offset field values. As a result, the target computer is unable to reassemble these packets and is forced to crash, hang, or reboot.

In a ping of death attack, the attacker sends an ICMP packet larger than 65,536 bytes. Since the operating system does not know how to handle a packet larger than 65,536 bytes, it either freezes or crashes at the time of reassembling the packet. However, nowadays the operating systems discard such packets, so the ping of death attack is not applicable under these circumstances.

Answer option B is incorrect. A SYN flood is a form of Denial-of-Service (DoS) attack in which an attacker sends a succession of SYN requests to a target's system. When a client attempts to start a TCP connection to a server, the client and server exchange a series of messages, which normally runs as follows:

1. The client requests a connection by sending a SYN (synchronize) message to the server.

2. The server acknowledges this request by sending SYN-ACK back to the client.

3. The client responds with an ACK (acknowldgement), and the connection is established.

The attack occurs when the attacker sends thousands and thousands of SYN packets to the victim, forcing the victim to wait for replies that never come. While the host is waiting for so many replies, it cannot accept any requests, so it becomes unavailable.

Answer option D is incorrect. In a land attack, the attacker sends a spoofed TCP SYN packet in which the IP address of the target is filled in both the source and destination fields. On receiving the spoofed packet, the target system becomes confused and goes into a frozen state. Now-a-days, antivirus can easily detect such an attack.

A5. Answer option B is correct.

A Denial-of-Service (DoS) attack is mounted with the objective of causing a negative impact on the performance of a computer or network. It is also known as a network saturation attack or bandwidth consumption attack. Attackers perform DoS attacks by sending a large number of protocol packets to the network. The effects of a DoS attack are as follows:

- Saturates network resources

- Disrupts connections between two computers, thereby preventing communications between services

- Disrupts services to a specific computer

- Causes failure to access a Web site

- Results in an increase in the amount of spam

A Denial-of-Service attack is very common on the Internet because it is much easier to accomplish. Most of the DoS attacks rely on the weaknesses in the TCP/IP protocol.

Answer option A is incorrect. Replay attack is a type of attack in which attackers capture packets containing passwords or digital signatures whenever packets pass between two hosts on a network. In an attempt to obtain an authenticated connection, the attackers then resend the captured packet to the system.

Answer option C is incorrect. Address Resolution Protocol (ARP) spoofing, also known as ARP poisoning or ARP Poison Routing (APR), is a technique used to attack an Ethernet wired or wireless network. ARP spoofing may allow an attacker to sniff data frames on a local area network (LAN), modify the traffic, or stop the traffic altogether. The attack can only be used on networks that actually make use of ARP and not another method of address resolution. The principle of ARP spoofing is to send fake ARP messages to an Ethernet LAN. Generally, the aim is to associate the attacker's MAC address with the IP address of another node (such as the default gateway). Any traffic meant for that IP address would be mistakenly sent to the attacker instead. The attacker could then choose to forward the traffic to the actual default gateway (passive sniffing) or modify the data before forwarding it. ARP spoofing attacks can be run from a compromised host, or from an attacker's machine that is connected directly to the target Ethernet segment.

Answer option D is incorrect. The rainbow attack is the fastest method of password cracking. This method of password cracking is implemented by calculating all the possible hashes for a set of characters and then storing them in a table known as the Rainbow table. These password hashes are then employed to the tool that uses the Rainbow algorithm and searches the Rainbow table until the password is not fetched.

Chapter 9 - Investigating Corporate Espionage, Trade marks and Copyright Infringement

Overview

Cyber law is a very wide term, which wraps up the legal issue related to use of communicative, transactional, and distributive aspect of networked information device and technologies. It is commonly known as INTERNET LAW. These laws are important to apply, as Internet does not tend to make any geographical and jurisdictional boundaries clear; this is the reason why Cyber law is not very efficient.

Cyber laws came into existence in the early 90's. They were formulated to prevent the growing chaos and crime in cyber space. The laws of a nation may have extraterritorial impact extending the jurisdiction beyond the sovereign and territorial limits of that nation. This is particularly problematic as the medium of the Internet does not explicitly recognize sovereignty and territorial limitations. There is no uniform, international jurisdictional law of universal application, and such questions are generally a matter of conflict of laws, particularly private international law. An example would be where the contents of a Web site are legal in one country and illegal in another. In the absence of a uniform jurisdictional code, legal practitioners are generally left with a conflict of law issue.

Key Points

Understanding Corporate Espionage.

- The Espionage Act of 1917 was a United States federal law passed shortly after entering World War I, on June 15, 1917, which made it a crime for a person:

- To convey information with intent to interfere with the operation or success of the armed forces of the United States or to promote the success of its enemies. This was punishable by death or by imprisonment for not more than 30 years.

- To convey false reports or false statements with intent to interfere with the operation or success of the military or naval forces of the United States or to promote the success of its enemies and whoever when the United States is at war, to cause or attempt to cause insubordination, disloyalty, mutiny, refusal of duty, in the military or naval forces of the United States, or to willfully obstruct the recruiting or enlistment service of the United States.

- The Economic Espionage Act of 1996 makes the theft or misappropriation of a trade secret a federal crime. Unlike Espionage, which is governed by Title 18 U.S. Code Sections 792 - 799, the offense involves commercial information, not classified or national defense information. This law contains two sections criminalizing two sorts of activity. The first, 18 U.S.C. 1831(a), criminalizes the misappropriation of trade secrets (including conspiracy to misappropriate trade secrets and the subsequent acquisition of such misappropriated trade secrets) with the knowledge or intent that the theft will benefit a foreign power. The second section, 18 U.S.C. 1832, criminalizes the misappropriation of trade secrets related to or included in a product that is produced for or placed in interstate (including international) commerce, with the knowledge or intent that the misappropriation will injure the owner of the trade secret.

- The Electronic Communications Privacy Act of 1986 (ECPA) was enacted by the United States Congress to extend government restrictions on wire taps from telephone calls to include transmissions of electronic data by computer. Specifically, ECPA was an amendment to Title III of the Omnibus Crime Control and Safe Streets Act of 1968 (the Wiretap Statute), which was primarily designed to prevent unauthorized government access to private electronic communications. The ECPA also added new provisions prohibiting access to stored electronic communications, i.e., the Stored Communications Act,18 U.S.C. 2701-2712. The ECPA also included so-called pen/trap provisions that permit the tracing of telephone communications. Section 2709 of the Act allows the FBI to issue National Security Letters (NSLs) to Internet service providers (ISPs) ordering them to disclose records about their customers.

- The Wiretap Act (18 U.S.C. 2510) is a sequence of title III of the Omnibus Crime Control and Safe Streets Act of 1968. It makes it illegal for anyone to intercept or disclose intercepted telephone communications, unless so ordered by a court of competent jurisdiction. In order to protect the integrity of the courts while also ensuring the privacy of citizens was not violated the Act provided a legal framework within which wiretaps and interceptions of communications could be used. The Act requires a court order authorizing the use of such measures against U.S. citizens, with penalties for those who do not get such authorization.

- The Computer Fraud and Abuse Act is a law passed by the United States Congress in 1984 intended to reduce cracking of computer systems and to address federal computer-related offenses. The Computer Fraud and Abuse Act (codified as 18 U.S.C. 1030) governs cases with a compelling federal interest, where computers of the federal government or certain financial institutions are involved, where the crime itself is interstate in nature, or computers used in interstate and foreign commerce. It was amended in 1986, 1994, 1996, in 2001 by the USA PATRIOT Act, and in 2008 by the Identity Theft Enforcement and Restitution Act. Section (b) of the act punishes anyone who not just commits or attempts to commit an offense under the Computer Fraud and Abuse Act but also those who conspire to do so.

- Corporate espionage is the espionage conducted for commercial purposes instead of national security purposes. The term is distinct from legal and ethical activities such as examining corporate publications, Websites, patent filings, and the like to determine the activities of a corporation. Theoretically the difference between espionage and legal information gathering is clear. In practice, it is quite difficult to sometimes tell the difference between legal and illegal methods. Especially if one starts to consider the ethical side of information gathering, the border becomes even more blurred and elusive of definition. Industrial espionage describes activities such as theft of trade secrets, bribery, blackmail, and technological surveillance.

- The Economic Espionage Act of 1996 makes the theft or misappropriation of a trade secret a federal crime. Unlike Espionage, which is governed by Title 18 U.S. Code Sections 792-799, the offense involves commercial information, not classified or national defense information. This law contains two sections criminalizing two sorts of activity.

- Section 2709 of the Electronic Communications Privacy Act of 1986 allows the FBI to issue National Security Letters (NSLs) to Internet service providers (ISPs) ordering them to disclose records about their customers.

- For the successful prosecution of the corporate espionage, it is mandatory to prove that the information has value. This value can be a monetary value, a hidden value, or an economic advantage to the competitor company.

- A keystroke logger records everything a person types using the keyboard.

- Data diddling involves changing data prior to or during input to a computer in an effort to commit fraud.

Pop Quiz

Q1: Which of the following firewalls depends on the three-way handshake of the TCP protocol?

Ans: Stateful firewall

Q2: Which of the following tools is used to collect volatile data over a network?

Ans: Netcat

Laws Copyright and Trademark

- The Trademark law is a piece of legislation that contains the federal statutes of trademark law in the United States. The Act prohibits a number of activities, including trademark infringement, trademark dilution, and false advertising. Trademarks were traditionally protected in the United States only under State common law, growing out of the tort of unfair competition. Trademark law in the United States is almost entirely enforced through private lawsuits. The exception is in the case of criminal counterfeiting of goods. Otherwise, the responsibility is entirely on the mark owner to file suit in either state or federal civil court in order to restrict an infringing use. Failure to "police" a mark by stopping infringing uses can result in the loss of protection.

- Copyright law of the United States governs the legally enforceable rights of creative and artistic works under the laws of the United States. Copyright law in the United States is part of federal law, and is authorized by the U.S. Constitution. The power to enact copyright law is granted in Article I, Section 8, Clause 8, also known as the Copyright Clause. This clause forms the basis for U.S. copyright law ("Science", "Authors", "Writings") and patent law ("useful Arts", "Inventors", "Discoveries"), and includes the limited terms (or durations) allowed for copyrights and patents ("limited Times"), as well as the items they may protect. In the U.S., registrations of claims of copyright, recordation of copyright transfers, and other administrative aspects of copyright are the responsibility of the United States Copyright Office, a part of the Library of Congress.

- A patent is a set of exclusive rights granted by a state to an inventor or his assignee for a fixed period of time in exchange for the disclosure of an invention.

- A trade secret is a formula, practice, process, design, instrument, pattern, or compilation of information by which a business can obtain an economic advantage over its competitors or customers, and which is not generally known.

- A trademark is a name, symbol, or slogan with which a product is identified. Its uniqueness makes the product noticeable among the same type of products.

- Monitoring the computer hard disks or e-mails of employees pertains to the privacy policy of an organization.

- Chain of custody should be documented to preserve evidences for presentation in court.

- The Trademark law is a piece of legislation that contains the federal statutes of trademark law in the United States.

- The following steps are generally followed in computer forensic examinations: acquire, authenticate, and acquire.

Pop Quiz

Q1: Which of the following firewalls depends on the three-way handshake of the TCP protocol?

Ans: Stateful firewall

Q2: Which of the following Linux/UNIX commands is used to delete files permanently so that the files cannot be recovered?

Ans: Shred

- Dumpster diving refers to going through someone's trash to find out useful or confidential information.

- A patent enables an inventor to legally enforce his right to exclude others from using his invention.

- Wiretapping is generally practiced by the police or any other recognized governmental authority.

- Eavesdropping can be done over telephone lines (wiretapping), e-mail, instant messaging, and any other method of communication considered private.

Different Detection Tools

- JPlag is a software plagiarism detection system. It examines program structure and uses knowledge about programming language syntax to detect plagiarism across multiple source files. JPlag currently supports Java, C#, C, C++, Scheme, and natural language text. It detects similarities between students' source code files and the commonalities with instructor-provided code. A quantitative score determines the degree of similarity with another piece of work and can help to assess the likely time taken by and understanding of the student.

- Plagiarism is defined as the "use or close imitation of the language and thoughts of another author and the representation of them as one's own original work." While plagiarism in scholarship and journalism has a centuries-old history, the development of the Internet, where articles appear as electronic text, has made the physical act of copying the work of others much easier. Plagiarism is not copyright infringement. While both terms may apply to a particular act, they are different transgressions. Copyright infringement is a violation of the rights of a copyright holder, when material protected by copyright is used without consent. On the other hand, plagiarism is concerned with the unearned increment to the plagiarizing author's reputation that is achieved through false claims of authorship.

- Turnitin is an Internet-based plagiarism-detection service created by iParadigms, LLC. Institutions, typically universities and high schools, buy licenses to submit essays to the Turnitin Website, which checks the document for plagiarism. Students may be required by schools to submit essays to Turnitin, as a deterrent to plagiarism. This has been a source of criticism, with some students refusing to do so in the belief that requiring it constitutes a presumption of guilt. Additionally, critics have alleged that use of the software violates educational privacy and intellectual property laws.

- A host-based intrusion detection system (HIDS) is an intrusion detection system that monitors and analyses the internals of a computing system rather than the network packets on its external interfaces. A host-based Intrusion Detection System (HIDS) monitors all or parts of the dynamic behavior and the state of a computer system. HIDS look at the state of a system, its stored information, whether in RAM, in the file system, log files or elsewhere; and check that the contents of these appear as expected.

- A network intrusion detection system (NIDS) is an intrusion detection system that tries to detect malicious activity such as denial of service attacks, port scans or even attempts to crack into computers by monitoring network traffic. A NIDS reads all the incoming packets and tries to find suspicious patterns known as signatures or rules. It also tries to detect incoming shell codes in the same manner that an ordinary intrusion detection systems does.

- A protocol-based intrusion detection system (PIDS) is an intrusion detection system, which is typically installed on a Web server, and is used in the monitoring and analysis of the protocol in use by the computing system. A PIDS will monitor the dynamic behavior and state of the protocol and will typically consist of a system or agent that would typically sit at the front end of a server, monitoring and analyzing the communication between a connected device and the system it is protecting. A typical use for a PIDS would be at the front end of a Web server monitoring the HTTP (or HTTPS) protocol stream.

- An application protocol-based intrusion detection system (APIDS) is an intrusion detection system that focuses its monitoring and analysis on a specific application protocol or protocols in use by the computing system. An APIDS will monitor the dynamic behavior and state of the protocol and will typically consist of a system or agent that would typically sit between a process, or group of servers, monitoring and analyzing the application protocol between two connected devices. A typical place for an APIDS would be between a Web server and the database management system, monitoring the SQL protocol specific to the middleware/business logic as it interacts with the database.

Pop Quiz

Q1: Which command used in Linux to create bit-stream images?

Ans:dd

Q2: Which sector on a hard disk contains codes that the computer uses to start the system?

Ans: Sector 0

- An Intrusion detection system (IDS) is software and/or hardware designed to detect unwanted attempts at accessing, manipulating, and/or disabling of computer systems, mainly through a network, such as the Internet. These attempts may take the form of attacks, as examples, by crackers, malware and/or disgruntled employees. An IDS cannot directly detect attacks within properly encrypted traffic. An intrusion detection system is used to detect several types of malicious behaviors that can compromise the security and trust of a computer system. This includes network attacks against vulnerable services, data driven attacks on applications, host based attacks, such as privilege escalation, unauthorized logins and access to sensitive files, and malware (viruses, trojan horses, and worms).

- John the Ripper (JTR) is a Password cracking tool that can work successfully on Unix and Linux environment as well as on Windows environment.

- JPlag is a software plagiarism detection system. It examines program structure and uses knowledge about programming language syntax to detect plagiarism across multiple source files. JPlag currently supports Java, C#, C, C++, Scheme, and natural language text.

- A host-based intrusion detection system (HIDS) is an intrusion detection system that monitors and analyses the internals of a computing system rather than the network packets on its external interfaces. It produces the false alarm because of the abnormal behavior of users and network.

Test Your Knowledge

Q1. Which of the following records everything a person types using the keyboard?

   A.   Line conditioner

   B.   Port scanner

   C.   Keystroke logger

   D.   Firewall

Q2. Which of the following involves changing data prior to or during input to a computer in an effort to commit fraud?

   A.   Eavesdropping

   B.   Spoofing

   C.   Wiretapping

   D.   Data diddling

Q3. Which of the following needs to be documented to preserve evidences for presentation in court?

   A.   Separation of duties

   B.   Chain of custody

   C.   Incident response policy

   D.   Account lockout policy

Q4. Adam works as a Computer Hacking Forensic Investigator for a garment company in the United States. A project has been assigned to him to investigate a case of a disloyal employee who is suspected of stealing design of the garments, which belongs to the company and selling those garments of the same design under different brand name. Adam investigated that the company does not have any policy related to the copy of design of the garments. He also investigated that the trademark under which the employee is selling the garments is almost identical to the original trademark of the company. On the grounds of which of the following laws can the employee be prosecuted?

A. Trademark law

B. Copyright law

C. Espionage law

D. Cyber law

Q5. Which of the following steps are generally followed in computer forensic examinations?

Each correct answer represents a complete solution. Choose three.

A. Analyze

B. Acquire

C. Encrypt

D. Authenticate

Answer Explanation

A1.   Answer option C is correct.

A keystroke logger records everything a person types using the keyboard.

Keystroke logging is a method of logging and recording user keystrokes. It can be performed with software or hardware devices. Keystroke logging devices can record everything a person types using his keyboard, such as to measure employee's productivity on certain clerical tasks. These types of devices can also be used to get usernames, passwords, etc.

Answer option A is incorrect. Line conditioner is a device that improves the ability of a communication line to transmit data. A line conditioner controls signal attenuation, noise, and distortion of the communication line.

Answer option B is incorrect. A port scanner is a software tool that is designed to search a network host for open ports. This tool is often used by administrators to check the security of their networks. It is also used by hackers to compromise the network and systems.

Answer option D is incorrect. A firewall is a tool to provide security to a network. It is used to protect an internal network or intranet against unauthorized access from the Internet or other outside networks. It restricts inbound and outbound access and can analyze all traffic between an internal network and the Internet. Users can configure a firewall to pass or block packets from specific IP addresses and ports.

A2.   Answer option D is correct.

Data diddling involves changing data prior to or during input to a computer in an effort to commit fraud. It also refers to the act of intentionally modifying information, programs, or documentations.

Answer option A is incorrect. Eavesdropping is the process of listening in private conversations. It also includes attackers listening in on the network traffic. For example, it can be done over telephone lines (wiretapping), e-mail, instant messaging, and any other method of communication considered private.

Answer option B is incorrect. Spoofing is a technique that makes a transmission appear to have come from an authentic source by forging the IP address, email address, caller ID, etc. In IP spoofing, a hacker modifies packet headers by using someone else's IP address to hide his identity. However, spoofing cannot be used while surfing the Internet, chatting on-line, etc. because forging the source IP address causes the responses to be misdirected.

Answer option C is incorrect. Wiretapping is an act of monitoring telephone and Internet conversations by a third party. It is only legal with prior consent. Legalized wiretapping is generally practiced by the police or any other recognized governmental authority.

A3.   Answer option B is correct.

A chain of custody should be documented to preserve evidences for presentation in court.

A chain of custody is a documentation that shows who has collected and accessed each piece of evidence. The documentation must be meticulously prepared including the minutest details (such as the date, time, location, and the verified identity of every person handling the evidence) so that the documentation is verifiable. It includes the time of accessing the evidence and the valid reason for doing so. A chain of custody must be maintained for all evidences in order to maintain the validity of the evidences.

Answer option A is incorrect. Separation of duties is the concept and a part of an organization's policy of having more than one person required to complete a task. It implements an appropriate level of checks and balances upon the activities of individuals. With the concept of SoD, business critical duties can be categorized into four types of functions: authorization, custody, record keeping, and reconciliation. In a perfect system, no person should handle more than one type of function. Separation of duties helps reduce the potential damage from the actions of one person. As an organization's policy it also helps to prevent collusion.

Answer option C is incorrect. Incident response policy is a document that defines an incident and helps people to respond appropriately to that incident. It provides information about people who are responsible for handling security incidents and how they can be contacted. The incident response policy also provides instructions to deal with documenting and disseminating incident-related information.

Answer option D is incorrect. Account Lockout policy locks out a user after a specified number of failed logon attempts. It prevents potential intruders from repeatedly trying different passwords to guess the correct password for accessing a user account.

A4. Answer option A is correct.

The Trademark law is a piece of legislation that contains the federal statutes of trademark law in the United States. The Act prohibits a number of activities, including trademark infringement, trademark dilution, and false advertising. Trademarks were traditionally protected in the United States only under State common law, growing out of the tort of unfair competition. Trademark law in the United States is almost entirely enforced through private lawsuits. The exception is in the case of criminal counterfeiting of goods. Otherwise, the responsibility is entirely on the mark owner to file suit in either state or federal civil court in order to restrict an infringing use. Failure to "police" a mark by stopping infringing uses can result in the loss of protection.

Answer option B is incorrect. Copyright law of the United States governs the legally enforceable rights of creative and artistic works under the laws of the United States. Copyright law in the United States is part of federal law, and is authorized by the U.S. Constitution. The power to enact copyright law is granted in Article I, Section 8, Clause 8, also known as the Copyright Clause. This clause forms the basis for U.S. copyright law ("Science",

"Authors", "Writings") and patent law ("useful Arts", "Inventors", "Discoveries"), and includes the limited terms (or durations) allowed for copyrights and patents ("limited Times"), as well as the items they may protect. In the U.S., registrations of claims of copyright, recordation of copyright transfers, and other administrative aspects of copyright are the responsibility of the United States Copyright Office, a part of the Library of Congress.

Answer option C is incorrect. The Espionage Act of 1917 was a United States federal law passed shortly after entering World War I, on June 15, 1917, which made it a crime for a person:

- To convey information with intent to interfere with the operation or success of the armed forces of the United States or to promote the success of its enemies. This was punishable by death or by imprisonment for not more than 30 years.

- To convey false reports or false statements with intent to interfere with the operation or success of the military or naval forces of the United States or to promote the success of its enemies and whoever when the United States is at war, to cause or attempt to cause insubordination, disloyalty, mutiny, refusal of duty, in the military or naval forces of the United States, or to willfully obstruct the recruiting or enlistment service of the United States.

Answer option D is incorrect. Cyber law is a very wide term, which wraps up the legal issue related to the use of communicative, transactional and distributive aspect of networked information device and technologies. It is commonly known as INTERNET LAW. These Laws are important to apply as Internet does not tend to make any geographical and jurisdictional boundaries clear; this is the reason why Cyber law is not very efficient. A single transaction may involve the laws of at least three jurisdictions, which are as follows:

1. The laws of the state/nation in which the user resides

2. The laws of the state/nation that apply where the server hosting the transaction is located

3. The laws of the state/nation, which apply to the person or business with whom the transaction takes place

A5. Answer options A, B, and D are correct.

The following steps are generally followed in computer forensic examinations:

1. Acquire: In this step, the examiner gets an exact duplicate copy of the original data for investigation. The examiner leaves the original copy intact.

2. Authenticate: In this step, the investigator shows that the data is unchanged and has not been tampered.

3. Analyze: In this step, the examiner analyzes data carefully. The examiner recovers evidence by examining hard disk drives, hidden files, swap data, the Internet cache, and the Recycle bin.

Answer option C is incorrect. Encrypt is not a step followed in computer forensic examinations.

Chapter 10 - Investigating Sexually harassment incident, Child Pornography

Overview

Child pornography refers to images or films (also known as child abuse images) and in some cases writings depicting sexually explicit activities involving a child; as such, child pornography is a record of child sexual abuse. Abuse of the child occurs during the sexual acts which are recorded in the production of child pornography,and the effects of the abuse on the child (and continuing into maturity) are compounded by the wide distribution and lasting availability of photographs of the abuse.

Key Points

Laws and Investigation of Sexual harassment.

- Quid pro quo sexual harassment is a type of sexual harassment in which a person is offered some kind of profit in exchange for sexual favors. In this type of harassment, a person can be offered a job, salary increase, promotion, etc. for sexual favors.

- When any incident of sexual harassment occurs, it is necessary that the records are maintained about the incident.

- Supervisors or employers of an organization should take some precautionary steps to avoid sexual harassment in workplace.

- The Civil Rights Act of 1991 is a United States statute that was passed in response to a series of United States Supreme Court decisions, which limited the rights of employees who had sued their employers for discrimination. The Act represented the first effort since the passage of the Civil Rights Act of 1964 to modify some of the basic procedural and substantive rights provided by federal law in employment discrimination cases. It provided for the right to trial by jury on discrimination claims and introduced the possibility of emotional distress damages, while limiting the amount that a jury could award. The 1991 Act also made technical changes in Civil Rights Act of 1964, affecting the length of time allowed to challenge unlawful seniority provisions, to sue the federal government for discrimination and to bring age discrimination claims, while allowing successful plaintiffs to recover expert witness fees as part of an award of attorney's fees and to collect interest on any judgment against the federal government.

- The Civil Rights Act of 1964 was a landmark piece of legislation in the United States that outlawed racial segregation in schools, public places, and employment. Conceived to help African Americans, the bill was amended prior to passage to protect women, and explicitly included white people for the first time. It also created the Equal Employment Opportunity Commission. In order to circumvent limitations on congressional power to enforce the Equal Protection Clause imposed by the Supreme Court in the Civil Rights Cases, the law was passed under the Commerce Clause, which had been interpreted by the courts as a broad grant of congressional power. Title VII of this Act prohibits discrimination against an individual because of his or her association with another individual of a particular race, color, religion, sex, or national origin. An employer cannot discriminate against a person because of his interracial association with another, such as by an interracial marriage.

- In the United States, Title VII of the 1964 Civil Rights Act was formulated to ensure safeguard of an employee from discrimination on the basis of race, color, religion, sex, and national origin. This law makes discrimination in employment illegal. Sexual discrimination is prohibited for both males and females. When this law was enacted it originally emphasized on the protection of woman in the work place.

- The Civil Rights Act of 1991 is a United States statute that was passed in response to a series of United States Supreme Court decisions which limited the rights of employees who had sued their employers for discrimination.

- Sexual Predators Act is enacted in United States in 1998, which prohibits and made illegal for an Internet Service Provider (ISP) to knowingly allow child pornography to appear on Web sites. It is necessary for an ISP to notify law enforcement that a Web site is hosted on its server, which contains child pornography material.

Pop Quiz

Q1: Which of the following tools is used to block email, Instant Message, Web site, or other media if inappropriate words such as pornography, violence etc. is used?

Ans: i ProtectYou

Q2: Which of the following laws prohibits and made illegal for an Internet Service Provider (ISP) to knowingly allow child pornography to appear on Web sites?

Ans: Sexual Predator Act

Effects and Prevention of Child Pornography

- Internet Crimes Against Children (ICAC) is a task-force started by the United States Department of Justice's Office of Juvenile Justice and Delinquency Prevention (OJJDP) in 1998. Its primary goals are to provide state and local law enforcement agencies the tools to prevent Internet crimes against children by encouraging multi-jurisdictional cooperation as well as educating both law enforcement agents and parents and teachers. The aims of ICAC task forces are to catch distributors of child pornography on the Internet, whether delivered on-line or solicited on-line and distributed through other channels and to catch sexual predators who solicit victims on the Internet through chat rooms, forums and other methods. Currently all fifty states participate in ICAC.

- Project Safe Childhood (PSC) is a Department of Justice initiative launched in 2006 that aims to combat the proliferation of technology-facilitated sexual exploitation crimes against children. PSC coordinates efforts by various federal, state and local agencies and organizations to protect children by investigating and prosecuting online sexual predators. PSC partners include Internet Crimes Against Children (ICAC) task forces, the FBI, U.S. Postal Inspection Service, Immigration and Customs Enforcement, the U.S. Marshals Service, the National Center for Missing & Exploited Children, and state and local law enforcement officials in each U.S. Attorney's district. PSC also helps local communities to create programs and develop strategies to investigate child exploitation.

- Hamachi is a zero-configuration virtual private network (VPN) shareware application capable of establishing direct links between computers that are behind NAT firewalls without requiring reconfiguration; in other words, it establishes a connection over the Internet that very closely emulates the connection that would exist if the computers were connected over a local area network. It is lightweight, high-performance, multi-platform, peer-to-peer virtual private networking system.

- Gnutella is Peer-to-Peer application, which is used to establish a file sharing network. It is the most popular file sharing network on the Internet with an estimated market share of more than 40%. The Gnutella network is a fully distributed alternative to such semi-centralized systems as FastTrack (KaZaA) and the original Napster. Method of searching on the Gnutella network is often unreliable. Each node is a regular computer user; as such, they are constantly connecting and disconnecting, so the network is never completely stable. Also, the bandwidth cost of searching on Gnutella would grow exponentially to the number of connected users, often saturating connections rendering slower nodes useless. Therefore, search requests would often be dropped, and most queries reached only a very small percentage of the network.

- Freenet is a decentralized, censorship-resistant distributed data store originally designed by Ian Clarke. Freenet aims to provide freedom of speech through a peer-to-peer network with strong protection of anonymity; as part of supporting its users' freedom, Freenet is free and open source software. Freenet works by pooling the contributed bandwidth and storage space of member computers to allow users to anonymously publish or retrieve various kinds of information. Freenet has been under continuous development since 2000; a version 1.0 has not yet been released but current builds are functionally usable.

- A peer-to-peer distributed network architecture is composed of participants that make a portion of their resources (such as processing power, disk storage, and network bandwidth) available directly to their peers without intermediary network hosts or servers. Peers are both suppliers and consumers of resources, in contrast to the traditional client-server model where only servers supply, and clients consume. Peer-to-peer was popularized by file sharing systems like Napster. Peer-to-peer file sharing networks have inspired new structures and philosophies in other areas of human interaction.

- Internet Crimes Against Children (ICAC) is a task-force started by the United States Department of Justice. Its primary goals are to provide state and local law enforcement agencies the tools to prevent Internet crimes against children by encouraging multi-jurisdictional cooperation as well as educating both law enforcement agents and parents and teachers.

- Persons who are sexually attracted towards child pornography often fall in one of the four different categories. These categories are as follows:

  - Passive pedophiles

  - Active pedophiles

  - Sexually indiscriminate

  - Sexually curious

- Hamachi, Gnutella and Freenet are Peer-to-Peer applications, which are used to network different computers together over the internet and provide file sharing capability.

- A federal judge of the United States in 1996 suggested a six-step method of evaluating images to find out whether the nude image of a child is considered to be child pornography. This six-step method is as follows:

  - Focal point was the child genitalia.

  - Setting of the visual deception is sexually suggestive.

  - Child is in inappropriate pose.

  - Child is fully or partially nude.

  - Visual depiction suggests willingness to engage in sexual activity.

  - Visual depiction intends to elicit a sexual response from the person viewing it.

Laws on Child Pornography

- Sexual Predators Act is enacted in United States in 1998, which prohibits and made illegal for an Internet Service Provider (ISP) to knowingly allow child pornography to appear on Web sites. It is necessary for an ISP to notify law enforcement that a Web site is hosted on its server, which contains child pornography material. This Web site or the pornographic contents of the Web site must be removed from the server immediately.

- The Child Pornography Prevention Act of 1996 (CPPA) was a United States federal law to restrict child pornography on the internet, including virtual child pornography. Before 1996, Congress defined child pornography with reference to the Ferber standard. In New York vs. Ferber, 458 U.S. 747 (1982), the Supreme Court held that the government could restrict the distribution of child pornography to protect children from the harm inherent in making it. The Child Pornography Prevention Act added two categories of speech to the definition of child pornography. The first prohibited "any visual depiction, including any photograph, film, video, picture, or computer or computer-generated image or picture" that "is, or appears to be, of a minor engaging in sexually explicit conduct." In Ashcroft case, the Court observed that this provision "captures a range of depictions, sometimes called 'virtual child pornography,' which include computer-generated images, as well as images produced by more traditional means." The second prohibited "any sexually explicit image that was advertised, promoted, presented, described, or distributed in such a manner that conveys the impression it depicts a minor engaging in sexually explicit conduct."

- The USA PATRIOT Act, commonly known as the "Patriot Act", is a statute enacted by the United States Government that President George W. Bush signed into law on October 26, 2001. The contrived acronym stands for Uniting and Strengthening America by Providing Appropriate Tools Required to Intercept and Obstruct Terrorism Act of 2001. The Act increases the ability of law enforcement agencies to search telephone, e-mail communications, medical, financial, and other records. It eases restrictions on foreign intelligence gathering within the United States and enhances the discretion of law enforcement and immigration authorities in detaining and deporting immigrants suspected of terrorism-related acts. The act also expands the definition of terrorism to include domestic terrorism, thus enlarging the number of activities to which the USA PATRIOT Act's expanded law enforcement powers can be applied.

- The Prosecutorial Remedies and Tools Against the Exploitation of Children Today Act (PROTECT Act) of 2003 is a United States law with the stated intent of preventing child abuse. The PROTECT Act incorporates the Truth in Domain Names Act (TDNA) of 2003 (originally two separate Bills, submitted by Senator Orrin Hatch and Congressman Mike Pence). The PROTECT Act is codified at 18 U.S.C. 2252(B)(b). This law provides mandatory life imprisonment of sex offenses against a minor if the offender has had a prior conviction of abuse against a minor with some exceptions.

- Innocent Images National Initiative (IINI) is an organization, which is developed by the FBI as part of its Cyber Crimes program. This organization is established for the purpose of identifying, investigating, and prosecuting people who use computers for sexual exploitation of children and child pornography. While performing these tasks, IINI also try to identify and release children being exploited.

- Anti-Child Porn.org (ACPO) is an organization, which has members all over the world, focusing on the topics related to child exploitation, online predators, and child pornography. Its Web site provides necessary information for law enforcement to parents, and other interested organizations. It also provides software such as Reveal, which can be used to evaluate and check files on a computer for explicit or illegal contents.

- Child Exploitation Tracking System (CETS) is a software based solution that aids law enforcement in managing and linking cases related to child protection. CETS was developed in collaboration with law enforcement. Administered by the loose partnership of Microsoft and law enforcement agencies, CETS offers law enforcement unique tools to gather and share evidence and information so they can identify, prevent and punish those who commit crimes against children.

- iProtectYou is a software, which is used for parental control and filtering. It controls what people, on a computer, accessing over the Internet. This tool can specify the access permission to users and groups on a computer. This tool also specifies words or phrases that will determine whether an email, Instant Message, Web site is blocked. It also block other sites that falls into specific categories, such as pornography, violence, etc. Certain newsgroups can also be blocked if they are not included in the database of child-safe groups.

Pop Quiz

Q1: Which anti-child pornography tool, which is used to organize, analyze, and share information related to child exploitation cases?

Ans: CETS

Q2: which software is used for parental control and filtering?

Ans: iportectYou

- Sexual Predators Act is enacted in United States in 1998, which prohibits and made illegal for an Internet Service Provider (ISP) to knowingly allow child pornography to appear on Web sites.

- Project Safe Childhood helps local communities to create programs and develop strategies to investigate child exploitation.

- Child Exploitation Tracking System (CETS) is an anti-child pornography tool, which is used to organize, analyze, and share information related to child exploitation cases.

Test Your Knowledge

Q1.   In which of the following types of sexual harassment a person is offered some kind of benefit in exchange for sexual favors or threat?

   A.   Quid pro quo sexual harassment

   B.   Hostile environment sexual harassment

   C.   Person-to-person sexual harassment

   D.   Visual sexual harassment

Q2.   Peter works as a Computer Hacking Forensic Investigator. He has been called by an organization to conduct a seminar to give necessary information related to sexual harassment within the work place. Peter started with the definition and types of sexual harassment. He then wants to convey that it is important that records of the sexual harassment incidents should be maintained, which helps in further legal prosecution. Which of the following data should be recorded in this documentation?

   Each correct answer represents a complete solution. Choose all that apply.

   A.   Date and time of incident

   B.   Location of each incident

   C.   Names of the victims

   D.   Nature of harassment

Q3.   Which of the following precautionary steps are taken by the supervisors or employers to avoid sexual harassment in workplace?

   Each correct answer represents a complete solution. Choose all that apply.

   A.   Communicate to an employee who is indulging in such behavior.

   B.   Establish a complaint mechanism.

C.   Immediately take action on the complaint.

D.   Contact the police and take legal action.

Q4.   In the United States, Title VII of the 1964 Civil Rights Act was formulated to protect an employee from discrimination on the basis of religion, color, race, national origin, and sex. This law makes discrimination in employment illegal. Which of the following was the original emphasis of the Act?

A.   Protect woman in the workplace

B.   Prevent child pornography

C.   Protect fundamental rights of an employee

D.   Equal position to all employees

Q5.   Which of the following Acts enacted in United States amends Civil Rights Act of 1964, providing technical changes affecting the length of time allowed to challenge unlawful seniority provisions, to sue the federal government for discrimination and to bring age discrimination claims?

A.   Civil Rights Act of 1991

B.   PROTECT Act

C.   The USA Patriot Act of 2001

D.   Sexual Predators Act

Answer Explanation

A1. Answer option A is correct.

Quid pro quo sexual harassment is a type of sexual harassment in which a person is offered some kind of profit in exchange for sexual favors. In this type of harassment, a person can be offered a job, salary increase, promotion, etc. for sexual favors.

Answer option B is incorrect. In hostile environment sexual harassment, unpleasant or offensive environment is created in a working place. This type sexual harassment is determined on the basis of whether a reasonable person is considering the work place to be hostile or not.

Answer options C and D are incorrect. All these options are not valid types of sexual harassment.

A2. Answer options A, B, and C are correct.

When any incident of sexual harassment occurs, it is necessary that the records are maintained about the incident. Data included in this documents are as follows:

- Date and time of incident

- Location of each incident

- Names of the victims

- Details of the incident

A3. Answer options A, B, and C are correct.

Supervisors or employers of an organization should take some precautionary steps to avoid sexual harassment in workplace. These steps are as follows:

- Communicate to an employee who is indulging in such behavior.

- Establish a complaint mechanism.

- Immediately take action on the complaint.

A4.   Answer option D is correct.

In the United States, Title VII of the 1964 Civil Rights Act was formulated to ensure safeguard of an employee from discrimination on the basis of race, color, religion, sex, and national origin. This law makes discrimination in employment illegal. Sexual discrimination is prohibited for both males and females. When this law was enacted it originally emphasized on the protection of woman in the work place. The Equal Employment Opportunity Act of 1972, which is added to the Civil Rights Act of 1964 includes public employees and grants enforcement authority to the Office of Personnel Management to guarantee non-discrimination in human resources actions and to establish positive employment measures.

A5.   Answer option A is correct.

The Civil Rights Act of 1991 is a United States statute that was passed in response to a series of United States Supreme Court decisions, which limited the rights of employees who had sued their employers for discrimination. The Act represented the first effort since the passage of the Civil Rights Act of 1964 to modify some of the basic procedural and substantive rights provided by federal law in employment discrimination cases. It provided for the right to trial by jury on discrimination claims and introduced the possibility of emotional distress damages, while limiting the amount that a jury could award. The 1991 Act also made technical changes in Civil Rights Act of 1964, affecting the length of time allowed to challenge unlawful seniority provisions, to sue the federal government for discrimination and to bring age discrimination claims, while allowing successful plaintiffs to recover expert witness fees as part of an award of attorney's fees and to collect interest on any judgment against the federal government.

Answer options B, C, and D are incorrect. All these Acts do not amends Title VII of Civil Rights Act of 1964.

The Prosecutorial Remedies and Tools Against the Exploitation of Children Today Act (PROTECT Act) of 2003 is a United States law with the stated intent of preventing child abuse. The PROTECT Act incorporates the Truth in

Domain Names Act (TDNA) of 2003 (originally two separate Bills, submitted by Senator Orrin Hatch and Congressman Mike Pence). The PROTECT Act is codified at 18 U.S.C. 2252(B)(b). This law provides mandatory life imprisonment of sex offenses against a minor if the offender has had a prior conviction of abuse against a minor with some exceptions.

The USA PATRIOT Act, commonly known as the "Patriot Act", is a statute enacted by the United States Government that President George W. Bush signed into law on October 26, 2001. The contrived acronym stands for Uniting and Strengthening America by Providing Appropriate Tools Required to Intercept and Obstruct Terrorism Act of 2001. The Act increases the ability of law enforcement agencies to search telephone, e-mail communications, medical, financial, and other records. It eases restrictions on foreign intelligence gathering within the United States and enhances the discretion of law enforcement and immigration authorities in detaining and deporting immigrants suspected of terrorism-related acts. The act also expands the definition of terrorism to include domestic terrorism, thus enlarging the number of activities to which the USA PATRIOT Act's expanded law enforcement powers can be applied.

Sexual Predators Act is enacted in United States in 1998, which prohibits and made illegal for an Internet Service Provider (ISP) to knowingly allow child pornography to appear on Web sites. It is necessary for an ISP to notify law enforcement that a Web site is hosted on its server, which contains child pornography material. This Web site or the pornographic contents of the Web site must be removed from the server immediately.

Chapter 11 - PDA, iPod, iPhone, and BlackBerry Forensics.

Overview

A personal digital assistant (PDA), also known as a palmtop computer, is a mobile device which functions as a Personal information manager and connects to the internet. The PDA has an electronic visual display enabling it to include a web browser, but some newer models also have audio capabilities, enabling them to be used as mobile phones or portable media players.

The iPod is a portable media player designed and marketed by Apple.

The iPhone is a line of Internet- and multimedia-enabled smartphones designed and marketed by Apple Inc.

BlackBerry is a line of mobile e-mail and smartphone devices developed by Canadian company Research In Motion (RIM).

Key Points

Features and Tools for PDA Forensics

- PDA investigative methods are pre-defined sequential steps, which should be used while performing a forensic investigation of a PDA. Four main steps, which are followed during forensic investigation of a PDA are as follows:

  1. Examination: In this step, potential sources of the evidence, which can be the device, the device cradle, the power supply, etc. is identified and collected. Any device that has synchronized with the PDA is also investigated in this step.

  2. Identification: In this step, the operating system that the device is using is identified. It may be possible that the device could be running on two operating systems. During the identification

process, many interfaces such as the cradle interface, the manufacturer serial number, the cradle type, and the power supply also helps in the investigation.

3. Collection: In this step, the data and potential evidence are collected from the memory devices that are part of the PDA. The power leads, cables, and any cradles that exist for the PDA is also collected in this step.

4. Documentation: In this step, documentation and "chain of custody" is maintained. These records must document the case number and the date and time PDA was collected. Important part of the documentation process is to produce a report that consists of the elaborated information that describes the entire forensic process.

- Dynamic dictionary files are keyboard caches used by the iPhone to learn particular dictionary of its owner. Whenever a user enters text whether usernames, certain passwords, website URLs, chat messages, email messages, or other form of input, it is stored in the keyboard cache.

Pop Quiz

Q1: Which of the following tools offers enhanced password protection in PDA?

Ans: PDA secure

Q2: Which of the following tools is used to search data and produce hash for integrity protection of the files acquired from PDA?

Ans:PDA Seizure

- Bluesnarfing is a rare attack in which an attacker takes control of a bluetooth enabled device. One way to do this is to get your PDA to accept the attacker's device as a trusted device.

- Blue jacking is the process of using another bluetooth device that is within range (about 30' or less) and sending unsolicited messages to the target.

- PDA investigative methods are pre-defined sequential steps, which should be used while performing a forensic investigation of a PDA.

Features and Tools for iPod and iPhone Forensics

- An iPod is a brand of portable media players designed and marketed by Apple Inc. and launched on October 23, 2001. The product line-up includes the hard drive-based iPod Classic, the touch screen iPod Touch, the video-capable iPod Nano, and the compact iPod Shuffle. The iPhone can function as an iPod but is generally treated as a separate product. iPod Classic models store media on an internal hard drive, while all other models use flash memory to enable their smaller size. As with many other digital music players, iPods can also serve as external data storage devices. Storage capacity varies by model.

- HFS Plus or HFS+ is a file system developed by Apple Inc. to replace their Hierarchical File System (HFS) as the primary file system used in Macintosh computers (or other systems running Mac OS). It is also one of the formats used by the iPod digital music player. HFS Plus is also referred to as Mac OS Extended, where its predecessor, HFS, is also referred to as Mac OS Standard.

- vCard is a file format standard for electronic business cards. iPod uses vCard file format to store contact information. vCards are often attached to e-mail messages, but can be exchanged in other ways, such as on the World Wide Web. They can contain name and address information, phone numbers, URLs, logos, photographs, and even audio clips.

- hCard is a microformat for publishing the contact details of people, companies, organizations, and places, in (X)HTML, Atom, RSS, or arbitrary XML. The hCard microformat does this using a 1:1 representation of vCard (RFC 2426) properties and values, identified using HTML classes and rel attributes. It allows parsing tools to extract the details, and display them, using some other Websites or mapping tools, index or search them, or to load them into an address-book program.

- The Linux kernel is an operating system kernel used by the Linux family of Unix-like operating systems. The term Linux distribution is used to refer to the various operating systems that run on top of the Linux kernel. The Linux kernel is released under the GNU General Public License version 2 (GPLv2) plus proprietary licenses for some controversial BLOBs and is developed by contributors worldwide; Linux is one of the most prominent examples of free / open source software. Early on, the MINIX community contributed code and ideas to the Linux kernel. At the time, the GNU Project had created many of the components required for a free software operating system, but its own kernel, GNU Hurd, was incomplete and unavailable. The BSD operating system had not yet freed itself from legal encumbrances. This meant that despite the limited functionality of the early versions, Linux rapidly accumulated developers and users who adopted code from those projects for use with the new operating system. The Linux kernel has received contributions from thousands of programmers.

- iPodLinux is a Clinux-based Linux distribution targeted specifically to run on Apple Inc.'s iPod. When the iPodLinux kernel is booted it takes the place of Apple's iPod operating system and automatically loads Podzilla. Podzilla is an alternative GUI and launcher for a number of additional included programs such as a video player, an image viewer, a command line shell, games, emulators for video game consoles, programming demos, and other experimental unfinished software. Many games, such as TuxChess, Bluecube, Chopper, StepMania, Doom, and Doom II can be played using iPodLinux. Recording through audio jack is at much higher quality in iPodLinux than Apple's firmware.

- The ARM Architecture is a 32-bit reduced instruction set computer (RISC) instruction set architecture (ISA) developed by ARM Holdings. The ARM architecture is the most widely used 32-bit ISA in terms of numbers produced. They were originally conceived as a processor for desktop personal computers by Acorn Computers, a market now dominated by the x86 family used by IBM PC compatible computers. The relative simplicity of ARM processors made them suitable for low power applications. The iPhone uses the ARM (advanced RISC machine) processor architecture, originally developed by ARM Ltd.

- Jailbreak is a process that allows iPhone and iPod Touch users to run any code on their devices, as opposed to only that code authorized by Apple. Once jailbroken, iPhone users are able to download many applications previously unavailable through the App Store via unofficial installers such as Cydia, Icy, and Installous, as well as illegal pirated apps. A jailbroken iPhone or iPod Touch is still able to use and update apps downloaded and purchased from Apple's official App Store. Jailbreaking, according to Apple, voids Apple's warranty on the device, although this is quickly remedied by restoring the device in iTunes.

- The disk layout of an iphone is divided into two partitions. The first partition is a 300 MB root partition, which is used to store the operating system and other preloaded applications used with the iPhone. This system partition is mounted as read-only by default. The remaining available space present as the second partition is assigned to the user partition, which is mounted as /private/var on the iPhone. All user data is stored in this partition.

- An iPhone is a line of Internet and multimedia-enabled smartphones designed and marketed by Apple Inc. It functions as a camera phone (also including text messaging and visual voicemail), a portable media player (equivalent to a video iPod), and an Internet client (with e-mail, Web browsing, and Wi-Fi connectivity). The user interface is built around the device's multi-touch screen, including a virtual keyboard.

- AFC (Apple File Connection) is the serial port protocol that is used by iTunes to transfer files to and from the iPhone and to send firmware-level commands. It is generally used for copying music and installing a software upgrade. This takes place over the device's USB dock connector, using a framework named MobileDevice, which gets installed with iTunes.

- SQLite is an ACID-compliant embedded relational database management system contained in a relatively small C programming library. The source code for SQLite is in the public domain. The iPhone makes heavy use of database files to store information such as address book contacts, SMS messages, email messages, and other data of a personal nature. This is done using the SQLite database software. SQLite databases typically have the file extension .sqlitedb, but some databases on the iPhone have the .db extension instead. A tool is required to access the data stored in these files.

- A property list is an XML-like configuration file used in the iPhone. Many preloaded applications, as well as Apple's operating system components, use property lists to store anything from basic configuration data to history and cache information. By analyzing these files, Adam can get an idea of what websites the criminal may have visited or what Google Maps direction lookups were queried. Other useful information may include mail server information, iTunes account info, etc.

- vCard is a file format standard for electronic business cards. iPod uses vCard file format to store contact information.

- For extensive analysis of the iPod, the Mac OS is preferred over Windows and other operating systems, because iPod have better interaction with the host machine running on Mac OS.

- iPodLinux is a Clinux-based Linux distribution targeted specifically to run on Apple Inc.'s iPod. When the iPodLinux kernel is booted it takes the place of Apple's iPod operating system and automatically loads Podzilla. Many games, such as TuxChess, Bluecube, Chopper, StepMania, Doom, and Doom II can be played using iPodLinux. Recording through audio jack is at much higher quality in iPodLinux than Apple's firmware.

- It is possible to determine the format of the drive from the iPod itself. This is achieved by selecting "Settings > About".

- It is possible to set iPod to read-only mode within Windows XP (SP2) by changing the registry key: HKEY_LOCAL_MACHINE\System\CurrentControlset\Control\StorageDevicePolicies. Setting this key to the hex value of 0x00000001 and restarting the computer will stop write access to any USB storage devices.

- When iPod is set up in computer using iTunes, a file named \iPod_Control\iTunes\DeviceInfo is created. This file contains the user name and the computer information. This information can be used to identify the user and computer that is used to initialize the iPod.

- An iPod has an internal clock, but the standard Apple's operating system for ipod does not update the file times. The standard iPod operating system records the time of the computer, with which it is connecting to. When iPod is using alternative operating system such as iPod Linux, the internal system clock of the iPod updates the file times.

- AFC (Apple File Connection) is the serial port protocol that is used by iTunes to transfer files to and from the iPhone and to send firmware-level commands.

- By placing the device into restore mode will stop the iPhone from booting temporarily. All data will remain intact and safe.

Pop Quiz

Q1: Which of the following Apple's ipod uses only the FAT32 file system?

Ans:iPod Shuffle

Q2: Which of the following is deleted in the iPod restore process?

Ans:File Pointers

- A property list is an XML-like configuration file used in the iPhone. Many preloaded applications, as well as Apple's operating system components, use property lists to store anything from basic configuration data to history and cache information.

Working and Functions of Blackberry

- BlackBerry is a line of wireless handheld devices that was introduced in 1999 as a two-way pager. In 2002, the more commonly known smart phone BlackBerry was released, which supports push e-mail, mobile telephone, text messaging, internet faxing, Web browsing and other wireless information services as well as a multi-touch interface. It is an example of a convergent device. While including PDA applications (address book, calendar, to-do lists, etc.) as well as telephone capabilities on newer models, the BlackBerry is primarily known for its ability to send and receive e-mail wherever it can access a wireless network of certain cellular phone carriers.

- Push technology, or server push, describes a style of Internet-based communication where the request for a given transaction is initiated by the publisher or central server. It is contrasted with pull technology, where the request for the transmission of information is initiated by the receiver or client. Push services are often based on information preferences expressed in advance. This is called a publish/subscribe model. A client might subscribe to various information channels. Whenever new content is available on one of those channels, the server would push that information out to the user. The BlackBerry was the first popular example of push technology for email in a wireless context.

- A wireless LAN (WLAN) is a wireless local area network that links two or more computers or devices using spread-spectrum or OFDM modulation technology based to enable communication between devices in a limited area. This gives users the mobility to move around within a broad coverage area and still be connected to the network.

- Infrared technology is used to establish a wireless communication between two devices (generally mobile phones) placed in a free line of sight. Infrared radiation lies between microwaves and the visible light in the electromagnetic spectrum. LED transmits the infrared signal as a pulse of non-visible light in the infrared communication. At the reception end, sensor detects and captures the infrared signal, which are then processed to acquire the information infrared signals contains.

- BlackBerry operating system is the proprietary software platform made by Research In Motion for its BlackBerry line of handhelds. BlackBerry operating system provides multi-tasking, and makes heavy use of the device's specialized input devices, particularly the trackball or touch screen. The current version of BlackBerry operating system provides a subset of MIDP 2.0, and allows over-the-air activation and synchronization with Microsoft Outlook, calendar, tasks, notes and contacts. It also provides a password keeper program to store sensitive information.

- Triple DES is the common name for the Triple Data Encryption Algorithm (TDEA). It is so named because it applies the Data Encryption Standard (DES) cipher algorithm three times to each data block. The Data Encryption Standard (DES) is a block cipher (a form of shared secret encryption), which is based on a symmetric-key algorithm that uses a 56-bit key. The algorithm was initially controversial with classified design elements, a relatively short key length, and suspicions about a National Security Agency (NSA) backdoor. Triple DES provides a relatively simple method of increasing the key size of DES to protect against brute force attacks, without requiring a completely new block cipher algorithm.

- Advanced Encryption Standard (AES) is an encryption standard adopted by the U.S. government. The standard comprises three block ciphers, AES-128, AES-192 and AES-256, adopted from a larger collection originally published as Rijndael. AES is based on a design principle known as a Substitution permutation network. It is fast in both software and hardware. It is relatively easy to implement, and requires little memory. Unlike its predecessor DES, AES does not use a Feistel network. AES has a fixed block size of 128 bits and a key size of 128, 192, or 256 bits, whereas Rijndael can be specified with block and key sizes in any multiple of 32 bits, with a minimum of 128 bits and a maximum of 256 bits. Assuming one byte equals 8 bits, the fixed block size of 128 bits is 128 8 = 16 bytes. AES operates on a 4 4 array of bytes, termed the state. Most AES calculations are done in a special finite field.

- The AES cipher is specified as a number of repetitions of transformation rounds that convert the input plain-text into the final output of cipher-text. Each round consists of several processing steps, including one that depends on the encryption key. A set of reverse rounds are applied to transform cipher-text back into the original plain-text using the same encryption key.

- RSA (which stands for Rivest, Shamir, and Adleman) is an algorithm for public-key cryptography. It is the first algorithm known to be suitable for signing as well as encryption, and one of the first great advances in public key cryptography. RSA is widely used in electronic commerce protocols, and is believed to be secure given sufficiently long keys and the use of up-to-date implementations.

- Evidence collection in BlackBerry is totally different from the traditional evidence collection methods of forensic investigators. In BlackBerry, different log files are taken in account before taking the image. Once the log information is retrieved and processed, image is taken. Log files, which are used to collect evidences in BlackBerry are as follows:

  o Radio status: This log helps to enumerate the state of the radio functions of the device.

  o Roam and Radio: This log has a buffer of maximum 16 entries. It records information related to the tower, channel, etc.

  o Transmit/Receive: This log is used to record gateway information and the type and size of data transmitted.

- o Profile string: This log comprises the information of the negotiation with the last utilized radio tower.

- Unit control functions are used to review the different logs present in BlackBerry. These logs are not accessed by the standard user interface. Different unit control functions are as follows:

  - o Mobitex2 Radio status: This unit control function provides information about four logs, which are as follows:

  - o Radio status: This log helps to enumerate the state of the radio functions of the device.

  - o Roam & Radio: This log has a buffer of maximum 16 entries. It records information related to the tower, channel, etc.

  - o Transmit/Receive: This log is used to record gateway information and the type and size of data transmitted.

  - o Profile String: This log comprises the information of the negotiation with the last utilized radio tower.

  - o Device status: This unit control function provides information about different devices, port status etc.

  - o Battery Status: This unit control function provides information about battery type, battery load, battery status, and temperature.

  - o Free Mem: This unit control function provides information about memory allocation and the largest free blocks.

  - o WatchPuppy: This unit control function logs an entry when certain application uses the CPU after predetermined threshold and kills the processes that do not release the CPU.

- By using Push technology, BlackBerry does not requires some form of desktop synchronization like the PDA does.

- The current version of BlackBerry operating system allows over-the-air activation and synchronization with Microsoft Outlook, calendar, tasks, notes and contacts. It also provides a password keeper program to store sensitive information.

Pop Quiz

Q1: Which of the following protocols is used by BlackBerry to backup, restore, and synchronize the data that is communicated between the BlackBerry handheld unit and the desktop software?

Ans:BlackBerry Serial Protocol

Q2: Which of the following tools is used to access the log files in BlackBerry provided by BlackBerry itself?

Ans: Software Development Toolkit (SDK)

- The BlackBerry has two encryption options; Triple Data Encryption Standard (DES) and the Advance Encryption Standard (AES).

- The BlackBerry is an always-on, push messaging device, which can push information any time. This push data has a capability to overwrite any data that was deleted previously.

- Evidence collection in BlackBerry is totally different from the traditional evidence collection methods of forensic investigators. In BlackBerry, different log files are taken in account before taking the image. Once the log information is retrieved and processed, image is taken.

- Unit control functions are used to review the different logs present in the BlackBerry. These logs are not accessed by the standard user interface.

Investigative Reports

- An expert witness or professional witness is a witness, who by virtue of education, training, skill, or experience, is believed to have knowledge in a particular subject beyond that of the average person, sufficient that others may officially (and legally) rely upon the witness's specialized (scientific, technical or other) opinion about an evidence or fact issue within the scope of their expertise. This opinion is referred to as the expert opinion. Expert witnesses may also deliver expert evidence about facts from the domain of their expertise. At times, their testimony may be rebutted with a learned treatise, sometimes to the detriment of their reputations.

- The Guidelines to write an investigative report is an important aspect, which should be kept in mind while writing a report. This helps in producing relevant and effective investigative report. These guidelines are as follows:

  - The report should be understandable by readers, who have no knowledge of the case and should be able to figure out what is written.

  - All ideas present in an investigative report should flow logically. The information present in an investigative report from facts to conclusions should be acknowledged in precise and balanced terms.

  - No assumption should be made about any facts while writing the investigative report.

  - Avoid spelling errors and poor grammar in the investigative report. Grammar and spellcheck tools can be used to avoid mistakes.

  - Investigative reports should always be written in active voice. Emotional words, judgmental words, and phrases should be avoided in an investigative report, when event is described.

- o   Investigative report should be written in brief and too much irrelevant data should not be included as it makes the report unclear.

- An investigative report is a document that is meant to provide information on a certain topic that is not easily obtained. It is meant to present the reader with a wealth of easily understood information and usually contains an interview or two on the subject. In order to write a successful investigative report, one must conduct a substantial amount of research and provide the reader with a wealth of information so that he or she can make an informed choice.

- Lay witness is a witness who is not qualified as an expert witness and generally excluded from testifying in the form of an opinion.

- The Guidelines to write an investigative report is an important aspect, which should be kept in mind while writing a report. This helps in producing relevant and effective investigative report.

- Section 2 of an investigative report includes the background and abstract of the investigative report. It consists of victim's allegations and optional information about the case. It also consists of the outcome of the case and the list of allegations.

- If any forensic investigation involves Computer in one way or another, then the investigation is coined as Computer Forensic Investigation. Development of technology from the last two decades is so rapid that it made lot easier for criminals to hide information about their crimes. One advantage enjoyed by investigators is that any type of Computer Crime results in some type of clue and evidence stored on computer but still there are number of Cyber Crimes, which require Computer Forensic investigation, some of them are as follows:

  - o   Unauthorized access

  - o   Property Theft (misuse of information)

o Forgery

o Privacy breach

o Computer fraud

o Child pornography

- First and Foremost step of Investigation process is Complaint. Investigation will never going to occur if it remains un-noticed, unless appropriate authorities are not aware of the crime being committed, criminal gets away with crime. Some fundamental steps involved in forensic investigation are as follows:

Flow of Methodology of Forensic Investigation

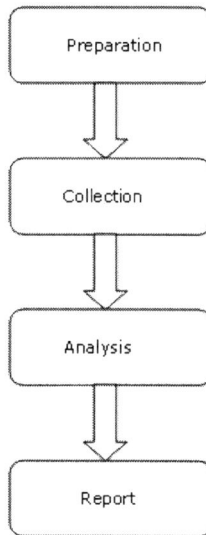

```
┌─────────────────────┐
│    Preparation      │
└─────────────────────┘
          ⬇
┌─────────────────────┐
│    Collection       │
└─────────────────────┘
          ⬇
┌─────────────────────┐
│    Analysis         │
└─────────────────────┘
          ⬇
┌─────────────────────┐
│    Report           │
└─────────────────────┘
```

- Preparation (of the investigator, not the data): Computer Forensic Investigators must be prepared with the tools and procedures used during investigation. These tools include Hardware as well as Software, which are used to secure evidence and data.

- Collection (the data): Next important step is to collect damaged data as efficiently as possible, damaged data typically includes deleted files, formatted hard disk, deleted partitions or any other form of electronic storage medium like compact disk, USB drives etc. Special care must be taken when handling computer evidence: most digital information is easily changed, and once changed it is usually impossible to detect that a change has taken place (or to revert the data back to its original state) unless other measures have been taken.

- Analysis: This step involves proper examination and evaluation of gathered information. During analysis, it is very important that the collected data and information aren't modified in any way, otherwise property of data will change. Therefore, it is very necessary to use tools that won't modify data. Chiefly Forensic Analysis consists of manual review of material on the media, reviewing the Windows registry for suspect information, discovering and cracking passwords, keyword searches for topics related to the crime, and extracting e-mail and images for review.

- Reporting: After the completion of Analysis, a detailed report is generated enlisting all possible evidences and information. This report is produced as a legal evidence before court whenever required.

Pop Quiz

Q1: Which of the following protocols is used by BlackBerry to backup, restore, and synchronize the data that is communicated between the BlackBerry handheld unit and the desktop software?

Ans:BlackBerry Serial Protocol

Q2: Which of the following tools is used to access the log files in BlackBerry provided by BlackBerry itself?

Ans: Software Development Toolkit (SDK)

Test Your Knowledge

Q1.   An executive in your company reports odd behavior on her PDA. After investigation you discover that a trusted device is actually copying data off the PDA. The executive tells you that the behavior started shortly after accepting an e-business card from an unknown person. What type of attack is this?

A.   Bluesnarfing

B.   PDA Hijacking

C.   Session Hijacking

D.   Privilege Escalation

Q2.   One of the sales people in your company complains that sometimes he gets a lot of unsolicited messages on his PDA. After asking a few questions, you determine that the issue only occurs in crowded areas like airports. What is the most likely problem?

A.   Blue snarfing

B.   Blue jacking

C.   A virus

D.   Spam

Q3.   Adam works as a professional Computer Hacking Forensic Investigator with the local police of his area. A project has been assigned to him to investigate a PDA seized from a local drug dealer. It is expected that many valuable and important information are stored in this PDA. Adam follows investigative methods, which are required to perform in a pre-defined sequential manner for the successful forensic investigation of the PDA. Which of the following is the correct order to perform forensic investigation of PDA?

A.   Examination, Identification, Collection, Documentation

B.   Examination, Collection, Identification, Documentation

C.   Identification, Collection, Examination, Documentation

D.   Documentation, Examination, Identification, Collection

Q4. Which of the following standard file formats is used by Apple's iPod to store contact information?

A.   vCard

B.   hCard

C.   HFS+

D.   FAT32

Q5. Adam works as a professional Computer Hacking Forensic Investigator. He works with the local police. A project has been assigned to him to investigate an iPod, which was seized from a student of the high school. It is suspected that the explicit child pornography contents are stored in the iPod. Adam wants to investigate the iPod extensively. Which of the following operating systems will Adam use to carry out his investigations in more extensive and elaborate manner?

A.   Windows XP

B.   Mac OS

C.   MINIX 3

D.   Linux

Answer Explanation

A1. Answer option A is correct.

Bluesnarfing is a rare attack in which an attacker takes control of a bluetooth enabled device. One way to do this is to get your PDA to accept the attacker's device as a trusted device.

Answer option B is incorrect. Though one might logically describe this as PDA hijacking, however, this term is not used.

Answer option C is incorrect. Session hijacking involves taking over a secure session between a client PC and a server.

Answer option D is incorrect. Privilege escalation involves logging in with a valid user account, but then getting additional privileges.

A2. Answer option B is correct.

Blue jacking is the process of using another bluetooth device that is within range (about 30' or less) and sending unsolicited messages to the target.

Answer option A is incorrect. Blue snarfing is a process whereby the attacker actually takes control of the phone. Perhaps copying data or even making calls.

Answer option C is incorrect. A virus would not cause unsolicited messages. Adware might, but not a virus.

Answer option D is incorrect. Spam would not be limited to when the person was in a crowded area.

A3. Answer option A is correct.

PDA investigative methods are pre-defined sequential steps, which should be used while performing a forensic investigation of a PDA. Four main steps, which are followed during forensic investigation of a PDA are as follows:

Examination:

In this step, potential sources of the evidence, which can be the device, the device cradle, the power supply, etc. is identified and collected. Any device that has synchronized with the PDA is also investigated in this step.

Identification:

In this step, the operating system that the device is using is identified. It may be possible that the device could be running on two operating systems. During the identification process, many interfaces such as the cradle interface, the manufacturer serial number, the cradle type, and the power supply also helps in the investigation.

Collection:

In this step, the data and potential evidence are collected from the memory devices that are part of the PDA. The power leads, cables, and any cradles that exist for the PDA is also collected in this step.

Documentation:

In this step, documentation and "chain of custody" is maintained. These records must document the case number and the date and time PDA was collected. Important part of the documentation process is to produce a report that consists of the elaborated information that describes the entire forensic process.

A4.   Answer option A is correct.

vCard is a file format standard for electronic business cards. iPod uses vCard file format to store contact information. vCards are often attached to e-mail messages, but can be exchanged in other ways, such as on the World Wide Web. They can contain name and address information, phone numbers, URLs, logos, photographs, and even audio clips.

Answer option B is incorrect. hCard is a microformat for publishing the contact details of people, companies, organizations, and places, in (X)HTML, Atom, RSS, or arbitrary XML. The hCard microformat does this using a 1:1 representation of vCard (RFC 2426) properties and values, identified using HTML classes and rel attributes. It allows parsing tools to extract the details, and display them, using some other Websites or mapping tools, index or search them, or to load them into an address-book program.

Answer option C is incorrect. HFS Plus or HFS+ is a file system developed by Apple Inc. to replace their Hierarchical File System (HFS) as the primary file system used in Macintosh computers (or other systems running Mac OS). It is also one of the formats used by the iPod digital music player. HFS Plus is also referred to as Mac OS Extended, where its predecessor, HFS, is also referred to as Mac OS Standard.

Answer option D is incorrect. The FAT32 file system is an enhancement of the FAT file system. It is more advanced and reliable than all the earlier versions of the FAT file system. It manages storage space on large hard disks more efficiently than the FAT16 file system. It uses a smaller cluster size than the FAT16 file system on the hard disk, thereby reducing the amount of space on the hard disk when users save small files. The FAT32 file system supports hard disk drives larger than 2GB and up to 2TB.

A5. Answer option B is correct.

For extensive analysis of the iPod, the Mac OS is preferred over Windows and other operating systems, because iPod have better interaction with the host machine running on Mac OS. When iPod is connected to a host machine running on Mac OS, it is formatted using Apple HFS+ file system. When it is connected using a host machine running on Windows operating system, it is formatted with FAT32 file system. The Apple HFS+ file system format provides more detailed meta-data, which gives the forensic investigator extensive and elaborated information than is supplied by the Windows FAT32 file system format. An iPod connected to a machine running on Mac OS provides more meta-data for analysis.

Section C

Full length Practice Test

Full Length Practice Test Questions

Q1. In which of the following access control models can a user not grant permissions to other users to see a copy of an object marked as secret that he has received, unless they have the appropriate permissions?

  A. Mandatory Access Control (MAC)

  B. Role Based Access Control (RBAC)

  C. Discretionary Access Control (DAC)

  D. Access Control List (ACL)

Q2. Which of the following types of attack can guess a hashed password?

  A. Brute force attack

  B. Evasion attack

  C. Denial of Service attack

  D. Teardrop attack

Q3. In which of the following security tests does the security testing team simulate as an employee or other person with an authorized connection to the organization's network?

  A. Local network

  B. Remote dial-up network

  C. Remote network

  D. Stolen equipment

Q4. Which of the following types of cyber stalking damage the reputation of their victim and turn other people against them by setting up their own Websites, blogs or user pages for this purpose?

  A. False victimization

  B. False accusations

  C. Encouraging others to harass the victim

  D. Attempts to gather information about the victim

Q5. Which of the following laws or acts, formed in Australia, enforces prohibition against cyber stalking?

    A.   Stalking Amendment Act (1999)

    B.   Malicious Communications Act (1998)

    C.   Stalking by Electronic Communications Act (2001)

    D.   Anti-Cyber-Stalking law (1999)

Q6. Which of the following statutes is enacted in the U.S., which prohibits creditors from collecting data from applicants, such as national origin, caste, religion etc?

    A.   The Electronic Communications Privacy Act

    B.   The Privacy Act

    C.   The Fair Credit Reporting Act (FCRA)

    D.   The Equal Credit Opportunity Act (ECOA)

Q7. Which of the following is the correct order of digital investigations Standard Operating Procedure (SOP)?

    A.   Request for service, initial analysis, data collection, data analysis, data reporting

    B.   Initial analysis, request for service, data collection, data analysis, data reporting

    C.   Request for service, initial analysis, data collection, data reporting, data analysis

    D.   Initial analysis, request for service, data collection, data reporting, data analysis

Q8. Which of the following representatives of incident response team takes forensic backups of the systems that are the focus of the incident?

    A.   Lead investigator

    B.   Legal representative

    C.   Information security representative

    D.   Technical representative

Q9. Which of the following types of firewall functions by creating two different communications, one between the client and the firewall, and the other between the firewall and the end server?

A.   Packet filter firewall

B.   Proxy-based firewall

C.   Stateful firewall

D.   Endian firewall

Q10. Which of the following IP addresses are private addresses?

Each correct answer represents a complete solution. Choose all that apply.

A.   10.0.0.3

B.   19.3.22.17

C.   192.166.54.32

D.   192.168.15.2

Q11. Which of the following hardware devices prevents broadcasts from crossing over subnets?

A.   Modem

B.   Bridge

C.   Router

D.   Hub

Q12. Peter, an expert computer user, attached a new sound card to his computer. He then restarts the computer, so that the BIOS can scan the hardware changes. What will be the memory range of ROM that the BIOS scan for additional code to be executed for proper working of soundcard?

A.   hAA43 to hF345

B.   hCA79 to hAC20

C.   hDF80 to hFF80

D.   hC800 to hDF80

Q13. Which of the following statements are NOT true about volume boot record or Master Boot Record?

Each correct answer represents a complete solution. Choose all that apply.

A. Volume boot sector is present at cylinder 0, head 0, and sector 1 of the default boot drive.

B. The actual program can be 512 bytes long.

C. The end of MBR marker is h55CC.

D. Four 16 bytes master partition records are present in MBR.

Q14. Which of the following files in LILO booting process of Linux operating system stores the location of Kernel on the hard drive?

A. /sbin/lilo

B. /boot/boot.b

C. /boot/map

D. /etc/lilo.conf

Q15. Adam works as a professional Computer Hacking Forensic Investigator. A project has been assigned to him to investigate the main server of SecureEnet Inc. The server runs on Debian Linux operating system. Adam wants to investigate and review the GRUB configuration file of the server system. Which of the following files will Adam investigate to accomplish the task?

A. /boot/grub/menu.lst

B. /boot/grub/grub.conf

C. /grub/grub.com

D. /boot/boot.conf

Q16. Mark works as a Network administrator for SecureEnet Inc. His system runs on Mac OS X. He wants to boot his system from the Network Interface Controller (NIC). Which of the following snag keys will Mark use to perform the required function?

A. C

B. D

C. N

D. Z

Q17. Which of the following modules of OS X kernel (XNU) provides the primary system program interface?

A.   Mach

B.   BSD

C.   I/O Toolkit

D.   LIBKERN

Q18 Allen works as a professional Computer Hacking Forensic Investigator. A project has been assigned to him to investigate a computer, which is used by the suspect to sexually harass the victim using instant messenger program. Suspect's computer runs on Windows operating system. Allen wants to recover password from instant messenger program, which suspect is using, to collect the evidence of the crime. Allen is using Helix Live for this purpose. Which of the following utilities of Helix will he use to accomplish the task?

A.   Mail Pass View

B.   MessenPass

C.   Asterisk Logger

D.   Access PassView

Q19. Trinity wants to send an email to her friend. She uses the MD5 generator to calculate cryptographic hash of her email to ensure the security and integrity of the email. MD5 generator, which Trinity is using operates in two steps:

Creates check file

Verifies the check file

Which of the following MD5 generators is Trinity using?

A.   Chaos MD5

B.   Mat-MD5

C.   Secure Hash Signature Generator

D.   MD5 Checksum Verifier

Q20. John works as a Network Administrator for We-are-Secure Inc. The company uses a Linux server. John wants to give the following file permissions to the imp.c file:

Read, Write, and Execute permissions to the owner

Read and Write permissions to groups

Read Only permissions to other users

Which of the following commands will John use to accomplish the task?

A.   chmod 764

B.   chmod 777

C.   chmod 712

D.   chmod 765

Q21. Which of the following switches is used with Pslist command on the command line to show the statistics for all active threads on the system, grouping these threads with their owning process?

A.   Pslist -t

B.   Pslist -m

C.   Pslist -x

D.   Pslist -d

Q22. Nathan works as a professional Ethical Hacker. He wants to see all open TCP/IP and UDP ports of his computer. Nathan uses the netstat command for this purpose but he is still unable to map open ports to the running process with PID, process name, and path. Which of the following commands will Nathan use to accomplish the task?

A.   Psloggedon

B.   Pslist

C.   fport

D.   ping

Q23. Which of the following tools is used to extract human understandable interpretation from the computer binary files?

A.   FAU

B.   Word Extractor

C.   Galleta

D.   FTK Imager

Q24.   John works as a professional Ethical Hacker. He has been assigned a project to test the security of www.we-are-secure.com. He wants to test the effect of a virus on the We-are-secure server. He injects the virus on the server and, as a result, the server becomes infected with the virus even though an established antivirus program is installed **on the server.** Which of the following do you think are the reasons why the antivirus installed on the server did not detect the virus injected by John?

Each correct answer represents a complete solution. Choose all that apply.

A.   John has changed the signature of the virus.

B.   John has created a new virus.

C.   The virus, used by John, is not in the database of the antivirus program installed on the server.

D.   The mutation engine of the virus is generating a new encrypted code.

Q25.   These are false reports about non-existent viruses. In these reports, the writer often claims to do impossible things. Due to these false reports, the network administrator shuts down his network, which in turn affects the work of the company. These reports falsely claim to describe an extremely dangerous virus, and declare that the report is issued by a reputed company. These reports are known as _____.

A.   Virus hoaxes

B.   Chain letters

C.   Spambots

D.   Time bombs

E.   Logic bombs

Q26.   In which of the following scanning techniques does a scanner connect to an FTP server and request that server to start data transfer to the third system?

A.   Bounce attack scanning

B.   Xmas Tree scanning

C.   TCP FIN scanning

D.   TCP SYN scanning

Q27. Adam, an expert computer user, doubts that virus named love.exe has attacked his computer. This virus **acquires** hidden and read-only attributes, so it is difficult to delete it. Adam decides to delete virus file love.exe from the command line. He wants to use del command for this purpose. Which of the following switches will he use with del command to delete hidden and read only-files?

A.   del /p /ar

B.   del /f /ah

C.   del /q /ar

D.   del /q

Q28. John used to work as a Network Administrator for We-are-secure Inc. Now he has resigned from the company for personal reasons. He wants to send out some secret information of the company. To do so, he takes an image file and simply uses a tool image hide and embeds the secret file within an image file of the famous actress, Jennifer Lopez, and sends it to his Yahoo mail id. Since he is using the image file to send the data, the mail server of his company is unable to filter this mail. Which of the following techniques is he performing to accomplish his task?

A.   Web ripping

B.   Social engineering

C.   Email spoofing

D.   Steganography

Q29. Which of the following tools can be used for steganography?

Each correct answer represents a complete solution. Choose all that apply.

A.   Image hide

B.   Snow.exe

C.   Stegbreak

D.   Anti-x

Q30. Which of the following tools is used to hide secret data in text files and is based on the concept that spaces and tabs are generally not visible in text viewers and therefore a message can be effectively hidden without affecting the text's visual representation for the casual observer?

A.   Image hide

B.   Snow.exe

C.   SARA

D.   Fpipe

Q31. Which of the following tools can be used to perform a whois query?

Each correct answer represents a complete solution. Choose all that apply.

A.   Sam Spade

B.   WsPingPro

C.   SuperScan

D.   Traceroute

Q32   Which of the following tools can be used to detect the steganography?

A.   Dskprobe

B.   Snow

C.   Blindside

D.   ImageHide

Q33. Which of the following statements are true about routers?

Each correct answer represents a complete solution. Choose all that apply.

A.   Routers are responsible for making decisions about which of several paths network (or Internet) traffic will follow.

B.   Routers organize addresses into classes, which are used to determine how to move packets from one network to another.

C.   Routers act as protocol translators and bind dissimilar networks.

D.   Routers do not limit physical broadcast traffic.

Q34. In a complex network, Router transfers data packets by observing some form of parameters or metrics provided in the routing table. Which of the following metrics is NOT included in the routing table?

A.   Bandwidth

B.   Frequency

C.   Delay

D.   Load

Q35. Which of the following tools are used to determine the hop counts of an IP packet?

Each correct answer represents a complete solution. Choose two.

A.   Ping

B.   Netstat

C.   TRACERT

D.   IPCONFIG

Q36. By gaining full control of router, hackers often acquire full control of the network. Which of the following methods are commonly used to attack Routers?

Each correct answer represents a complete solution. Choose all that apply.

A.   By launching Sequence++ attack

B.   By launching Max Age attack

C.   By launching Social Engineering attack

D.   Route table poisoning

Q37. Which of the following tools is an open source protocol analyzer that can capture traffic in real time?

A.   Snort

B.   NetWitness

C.   Netresident

D.   Wireshark

Q38.   You work as a professional Computer Hacking Forensic Investigator for DataEnet Inc. You want to investigate e-mail information of an employee of the company. The suspected employee is using an online e-mail system such as Hotmail or Yahoo. Which of the following folders on the local computer will you review to accomplish the task?

Each correct answer represents a complete solution. Choose all that apply.

A.   Cookies folder

B.   History folder

C.   Download folder

D.   Temporary Internet Folder

Q39.   Adam works on a Linux system. He is using Sendmail as the primary application to transmit e-mails. Linux uses Syslog to maintain logs of what has occurred on the system. Which of the following log files contains e-mail information such as source and destination IP addresses, date and time stamps etc?

A.   /var/log/logmail

B.   /var/log/mailog

C.   /log/var/mailog

D.   /log/var/logd

Q40.   Adam works as a professional Computer Hacking Forensic Investigator. He wants to investigate a suspicious email that is sent using a Microsoft Exchange server. Which of the following files will he review to accomplish the task?

Each correct answer represents a part of the solution. Choose all that apply.

A.   EDB and STM database files

B.   Checkpoint files

C.   cookie files

D.   Temporary files

Q41. Adam, a novice Web user is getting large amount of unsolicited commercial emails on his email address. He suspects that the emails he is receiving are the Spam. Which of the following steps will he take to stop the Spam?

Each correct answer represents a complete solution. Choose all that apply.

A.   Send an email to the domain administrator responsible for the initiating IP address.

B.   Forward a copy of the spam to the ISP to make the ISP conscious of the spam.

C.   Close existing email account and open new email account.

D.   Report the incident to the FTC (The U.S. Federal Trade Commission) by sending a copy of the spam message.

Q42. Which of the following can be applied as countermeasures against DDoS attacks?

Each correct answer represents a complete solution. Choose all that apply.

A.   Using Intrusion detection systems.

B.   Limiting the amount of network bandwidth.

C.   Using the network-ingress filtering.

D.   Blocking IP address.

E.   Using LM hashes for passwords.

Q43. Which of the following intrusion detection systems (IDS) produces the false alarm because of the abnormal behavior of users and network?

A.   Host-based intrusion detection system (HIDS)

B.   Network intrusion detection system (NIDS)

C.   Protocol-based intrusion detection system (PIDS)

D.   Application protocol-based intrusion detection system (APIDS)

Q44.   An organization monitors the hard disks of its employees' computers from time to time. Which policy does this pertain to?

A.   Privacy policy

B.   Backup policy

C.   Network security policy

D.   User password policy

Q45.   Which of the following steps are generally followed in computer forensic examinations?

Each correct answer represents a complete solution. Choose three.

A.   Analyze

B.   Acquire

C.   Encrypt

D.   Authenticate

Q46.   Which of the following refers to going through someone's trash to find out useful or confidential information?

A.   Hacking

B.   Dumpster diving

C.   Spoofing

D.   Phishing

Q47.   Which of the following enables an inventor to legally enforce his right to exclude others from using his invention?

A.   Patent

B.   Artistic license

C.   Phishing

D.   Spam

Q48.   Which of the following laws enacted in United States makes it illegal for an Internet Service Provider (ISP) to allow child pornography to exist on Web sites?

A.   Sexual Predators Act

B.   Child Pornography Prevention Act (CPPA)

C.   USA PATRIOT Act

D.   Prosecutorial Remedies and Tools Against the Exploitation of Children Today Act (PROTECT Act)

Q49. Which of the following anti-child pornography organizations helps local communities to create programs and develop strategies to investigate child exploitation?

A.   Project Safe Childhood (PSC)

B.   Internet Crimes Against Children (ICAC)

C.   Anti-Child Porn.org

D.   Innocent Images National Imitative (IINI)

Q50. Which of the following anti-child pornography tools is used to organize, analyze, and share information related to child exploitation cases?

A.   Child Exploitation Tracking System (CETS)

B.   iProtectyou

C.   Reveal

D.   Anti-Child Porn.org

Q51. In which of the following types of sexual harassment a person is offered some kind of benefit in exchange for sexual favors or threat?

A.   Quid pro quo sexual harassment

B.   Hostile environment sexual harassment

C.   Person-to-person sexual harassment

D.   Visual sexual harassment

Q52. Peter works as a Computer Hacking Forensic Investigator. He has been called by an organization to conduct a seminar to give necessary information related to sexual harassment within the work place. Peter started with the definition and types of sexual harassment. He then wants to convey that it is important that records of the sexual harassment incidents should be maintained, which helps in further legal prosecution. Which of the following data should be recorded in this documentation?

Each correct answer represents a complete solution. Choose all that apply.

A.   Date and time of incident

B.   Location of each incident

C.   Names of the victims

D.   Nature of harassment

Q53. Which of the following unit control functions logs an entry when certain application uses the CPU after predetermined threshold and kills the processes that do not release the CPU?

A.   WatchPuppy

B.   Mobitex2 radio status

C.   Device status

D.   Free Mem

Q54. Adam works as a professional Computer Hacking Forensic Investigator. He works with the local police. A project has been assigned to him to investigate an iPod, which was seized from a student of the high school. It is suspected that the explicit child pornography contents are stored in the iPod. Adam wants to investigate the iPod extensively. Which of the following operating systems will Adam use to carry out his investigations in more extensive and elaborate manner?

A.   Windows XP

B.   Mac OS

C.   MINIX 3

D.   Linux

Q55. Jason, a game lover, owns an Apple's iPod nano. He wants to play games on his iPod. He also wants to improve the quality of the audio recording of his iPod. Which of the following steps can Jason take to accomplish the task?

A.   Upgrade Apple's firmware.

B.   Install iPodLinux.

C.   Buy external add-ons.

D.   Install third party software.

Answer Explanation

A1.   Answer option A is correct.

Mandatory Access Control (MAC) is a model that uses a predefined set of access privileges for an object of the system. Access to an object is restricted on the basis of the sensitivity of the object and granted through authorization. Sensitivity of an object is defined by the label assigned to it. For example, if a user receives a copy of an object that is marked as "secret", he cannot grant permission to other users to see this object unless they have the appropriate permission.

Answer option B is incorrect. Role-based access control (RBAC) is an access control model. In this model, a user can access resources according to his role in the organization. For example, a backup administrator is responsible for taking backups of important data. Therefore, he is only authorized to access this data for backing it up. However, sometimes users with different roles need to access the same resources. This situation can also be handled using the RBAC model.

Answer option C is incorrect. The Discretionary access control (DAC) model has an access policy determined by the owner of an object. The owner decides who is allowed to access the object and what privileges they have.

Answer option D is incorrect. An access control list (ACL) model has a list of permissions attached to an object. The list specifies who or what is allowed to access the object and what operations are allowed to be performed on the object.

A2.   Answer option A is correct.

A hashed password can be guessed by brute force or dictionary attack.

In a brute force attack, an attacker uses software that tries a large number of the keys combinations in order to get a password. To prevent such attacks, users should create passwords more difficult to guess, e.g., using a minimum of six characters, alphanumeric combinations, and lower-upper case combinations, etc.

Answer option B is incorrect. An evasion attack is one in which an IDS rejects a malicious packet but the host computer accepts it. Since an IDS has rejected it, it does not check the contents of the packet. Hence, using this technique, an attacker can exploit the host computer. In many cases, it is quite simple for an attacker to send such data packets that can easily perform evasion attacks on an IDSs.

Answer option C is incorrect. A Denial-of-Service (DoS) attack is mounted with the objective of causing a negative impact on the performance of a computer or network. It is also known as a network saturation attack or bandwidth consumption attack. Attackers perform DoS attacks by sending a large number of protocol packets to the network. The effects of a DoS attack are as follows:

- Saturates network resources

- Disrupts connections between two computers, thereby preventing communications between services

- Disrupts services to a specific computer

- Causes failure to access a Web site

- Results in an increase in the amount of spam

A Denial-of-Service attack is very common on the Internet because it is much easier to accomplish. Most of the DoS attacks rely on the weaknesses in the TCP/IP protocol.

Answer option D is incorrect. In a teardrop attack, a series of data packets are sent to the target computer with overlapping offset field values. As a result, the target computer is unable to reassemble these packets and is forced to crash, hang, or reboot.

A3. Answer option C is correct.

In the local network security test, the security testing team simulates as an employee or other person who has an authorized connection to the organization's network.

The various modes of system security testing are as follows:

- Remote network: This mode attempts to simulate an attack launched over the Internet. The primary defenses that must be defeated in this test are border firewalls, filtering routers, etc.

- Remote dial-up network: This mode simulates an attack against the client's modem pools. The main targets of dial up testing are PBX units, Fax machines, and central voice mail servers. The primary defenses that must be defeated here are user authentication schemes.

- Local network: This test simulates an employee or other authorized person who has an authorized connection to the organization's network. The primary defenses that must be defeated here are intranet firewalls, internal Web servers, and server security measures.

- Stolen equipment: This mode simulates theft of a critical information resource such as a laptop owned by a strategist.

- Social engineering: This aspect attempts to check the integrity of the organization's employees.

- Physical entry: This test acts out a physical penetration of the organization's building. The primary defenses here are a strong security policy, security guards, access controls and monitoring, and security awareness.

  Security is a state of well-being of information and infrastructures in which the possibilities of successful yet undetected theft, tampering, and/or disruption of information and services are kept low or tolerable. The elements of security are as follows:

- Confidentiality: It is the concealment of information or resources.

- Authenticity: It is the identification and assurance of the origin of information.

- Integrity: It refers to the trustworthiness of data or resources in terms of preventing improper and unauthorized changes.

- Availability: It refers to the ability to use the information or resource as desired.

A4.   Answer option B is correct.

In false accusations, many cyberstalkers try to damage the reputation of their victim and turn other people against them. They post false information about them on Websites. They may set up their own Websites, blogs or user pages for this purpose. They post allegations about the victim to newsgroups, chat rooms or other sites that allow public contributions.

Answer option A is incorrect. In false victimization, the cyberstalker claims that the victim is harassing him/her.

Answer option C is incorrect. In this type of cyber stalking, many cyberstalkers try to involve third parties in the harassment. They claim that the victim has harmed the stalker in some way, or may post the victim's name and telephone number in order to encourage others to join the pursuit.

Answer option D is incorrect. In attempt to gather information, cyberstalkers may approach their victim's friends, family and work colleagues to obtain personal information. They may advertise for information on the Internet. They often will monitor the victim's online activities and attempt to trace their IP address in an effort to gather more information about their victims.

A5.   Answer option A is correct.

In Australia, the Stalking Amendment Act (1999) includes the use of any form of technology to harass a target as forms of criminal stalking. A person who commits the crime of unlawful stalking is liable to a maximum penalty of imprisonment for 5 years. However, a person is liable to a maximum penalty of imprisonment for 7 years if, for any of the acts constituting the unlawful stalking, the person intentionally threatens to use, violence against victim.

Answer option B is incorrect. Malicious Communications Act (1998) in the United Kingdom, classified cyber stalking as a criminal offense.

Answer option C is incorrect. Stalking by Electronic Communications Act (2001) is formed in Texas to prevent cyber stalking.

Answer option D is incorrect. Anti-Cyber-Stalking law is the first U.S. cyber stalking law went into effect in 1999 in California. Other states include prohibition against cyber stalking in their harassment or stalking legislation.

A6.   Answer option D is correct.

The Equal Credit Opportunity Act (ECOA) is a United States law (codified at 15 U.S.C. 1691 et seq.), enacted in 1974, that makes it unlawful for any creditor to discriminate against any applicant, with respect to any aspect of a credit transaction, on the basis of race, color, religion, national origin, sex, marital status, or age; to the fact that all or part of the applicant's income derives from a public assistance program; or to the fact that the applicant has in good faith exercised any right under the Consumer Credit Protection Act. The law applies to any person who, in the ordinary course of business, regularly participates in a credit decision, including banks, retailers, bankcard companies, finance companies, and credit unions.

Answer option A is incorrect. The Electronic Communications Privacy Act of 1986 (ECPA Pub. L. 99-508, Oct. 21, 1986, 100 Stat. 1848, 18 U.S.C. 2510) was enacted by the United States Congress to extend government restrictions on wire taps from telephone calls to include transmissions of electronic data by computer. Specifically, ECPA was an amendment to Title III of the Omnibus Crime Control and Safe Streets Act of 1968 (the Wiretap Statute), which was primarily designed to prevent unauthorized government access to private electronic communications. The ECPA also added new provisions prohibiting access to stored electronic communications, i.e., the Stored Communications Act, 18 U.S.C. 2701-2712.

Answer option B is incorrect. The Privacy Act of 1974, 5 U.S.C. 552a, establishes a code of fair information practice that governs the collection, maintenance, use, and dissemination of personally identifiable information about individuals that is maintained in systems of records by federal agencies. A system of records is a group of records under the control of an agency from which information is retrieved by the name of the individual or by some identifier assigned to the individual. The Privacy Act requires that agencies give the public notice of their systems of records by publication in the Federal Register. The Privacy Act prohibits the disclosure of information from a system of records of the subject individual, unless the disclosure is pursuant to one of twelve statutory exceptions.

Answer option C is incorrect. The Fair Credit Reporting Act (FCRA) is an American federal law (codified at 15 U.S.C. 1681 et seq.) that regulates the collection, dissemination, and use of consumer information, including consumer credit information. Along with the Fair Debt Collection Practices Act (FDCPA), it forms the base of consumer credit rights in the United States. It was originally passed in 1970, and is enforced by the US Federal Trade Commission.

A7. Answer option A is correct.

A standard operating procedure is a set of instructions having the force of a directive, covering those features of operations that lend themselves to a definite or standardized procedure without loss of effectiveness. Standard Operating Policies and Procedures can be effective catalysts to drive performance improvement and improve organizational results. Every good quality system is based on its standard operating procedures (SOPs). Steps of standard operating procedures are as follows:

- Request for service

- Initial analysis

- Data collection

- Data analysis

- Data reporting

Answer options B, C, and D are incorrect. All these are not the correct order of digital investigations Standard Operating Procedure (SOP).

Standard Operating Procedure (SOP) describes a best practice approach to executing tasks related to the production and maintenance of hardware and software, as well as incident and change management. There are a number of solutions available to automate the execution of SOPs for large enterprises, as it pertains to information technology, such as Creekpath, iConclude and Stratavia.

A8.   Answer option D is correct.

Technical representative creates forensic backups of the systems that are the focus of the incident, and provides valuable information about the configuration of the network and target system.

Answer option A is incorrect. Lead investigator acts as the manager of the computer security incident response team.

Answer option B is incorrect. Legal representative looks after the legal issue and ensures that the investigation process does not break any law.

Answer option C is incorrect. Information security representative informs about the security safeguards that may affect their ability to respond to the incident.

A9.   Answer option B is correct.

A proxy-based firewall running either on a dedicated hardware or as software on a general-purpose machine responds to input packets in the manner of an application, whilst blocking other packets.

Proxies make tampering with an internal system from the external network more difficult and misuse of one internal system would not necessarily cause a security breach exploitable from outside the firewall. Conversely, intruders may hijack a publicly-reachable system and use it as a proxy for their own purposes; the proxy then masquerades as that system to other internal machines. While use of internal address spaces enhances security, attackers may still employ methods such as IP spoofing to attempt to pass packets to a target network. The proxy firewall functions by maintaining two separate conversations, which are as follows:

- One between the client and the firewall

- One between the firewall and the end server

Answer options A, C, and D are incorrect. These firewalls do not function by creating two different communications.

A packet filter firewall is the basic system first generation firewall, which is a highly evolved and technical internet security feature now a days. Packet filters act by inspecting the "packets" which represent the basic unit of data transfer between computers on the Internet. If a packet matches the packet filter's set of rules, the packet filter will drop the packet, or reject it (discard it, and send "error responses" to the source). This type of packet filtering pays no attention to whether a packet is part of an existing stream of traffic (it stores no information on connection "state"). Instead, it filters each packet based only on information contained in the packet itself (most commonly using a combination of the packet's source and destination address, its protocol, and, for TCP and UDP traffic, the port number).

A stateful firewall is a firewall that keeps track of the state of network connections (such as TCP streams, UDP communication) traveling across it. The firewall is programmed to distinguish legitimate packets for different types of connections. Only packets matching a known connection state will be allowed by the firewall; others will be rejected.

The Endian Firewall is an open source Linux distribution that specializes on Routing/Firewalling and Unified Threat Management. It is being developed by the Italian Endian Srl and the community. Endian is originally based on IPCop, which itself was a fork of Smoothwall, but is now based on Linux From Scratch.

A10. Answer options A and D are correct.

The IP addresses 10.0.0.3 and 192.168.15.2 are private addresses.

The following table shows the address ranges for the private addresses used in different classes of networks:

Address Class Address Range

Class A	10.0.0.0 to 10.255.255.255
Class B	172.16.0.0 to 172.31.255.255
Class C	192.168.0.0 to 192.168.255.255

A11. Answer options C is correct.

Routers can be used to prevent broadcast storms from crossing over subnets, as they do not let broadcasts go forward. They interconnect networks and provide filtering functions. Routers route packets across multiple networks based on specific network addresses.

Answer option D is incorrect. A hub is a device used to link computers in a network. It connects computers that have a common architecture, such as Ethernet, ARCnet, FDDI, or Token Ring. All hub-computer connections for a particular network use the same type of cable, which can be twisted-pair, coaxial, or fiber-optic. Hubs are generally used in star topology networks. Token Ring hubs are also known as Multistation Access Units (MSAUs). A hub works on the physical layer of the OSI model.

Answer option B is incorrect. A bridge is an interconnectivity device that connects two local area networks (LANs) or two segments of the same LAN using the same communication protocols, and provides address filtering between them. Users can use this device to divide busy networks into segments and reduce network traffic. A bridge broadcasts data packets to all the possible destinations within a specific segment. Bridges operate at the data-link layer of the OSI model. Broadcasting each message to all the possible destinations would flood a network with unnecessary traffic.

Answer option A is incorrect. Modem stands for Modulator-Demodulator. It is a device that enables a computer to transmit information over standard telephone lines. Since a computer stores information digitally and a telephone line is analog, a modem converts digital signals to analog and vice versa. The conversion of a digital signal to analog is known as modulation and that of an analog signal to digital is known as demodulation.

A12. Answer option D is correct.

The BIOS scans memory for ROM in the range of hC800 to hDF80, which may contain any additional codes that are required to be executed for other adapter cards such as sound cards, RAID arrays, etc. If a ROM is found then the checksum is tested and programs found are run for each device. If the new device is found in this stage then the system displays the BIOS Setup screen, which allows making modifications in BIOS.

Answer options A, B, and C are incorrect. All these are not the correct memory ranges.

A13. Answer options B and C are correct.

The actual program can only be 444 bytes long. The end of MBR marker is h55AA.

Answer options A and D are incorrect. All these statements are true about MBR.

The Master Boot Sector (MBR) is a 512 bytes long boot sector that is the first sector of a default boot drive. It is also known as Volume Boot Sector, if the boot drive is un-partitioned. When the MBR is found, the program is tested and loaded to ensure that the last two bytes are h55AA. Actual program is only 444 bytes long.

A14. Answer options C is correct.

/boot/map file tells LILO where kernel is located on the drive. Kernel provides interface between the software and hardware components.

Answer option A is incorrect. /sbin/lilo is the kernel installer file in LILO booting.

Answer option B is incorrect. In LILO booting, /boot/boot.b file acts as the bootloader. This file displays menu of the available OS versions.

Answer option D is incorrect. /etc/lilo.conf file is the LILO configuration file.

A15. Answer option A is correct.

Adam will investigate and review "/boot/grub/menu.lst" file. This file is the GRUB configuration file of Debian Linux operating system.

Answer options B, C, and D are incorrect. All these files are not valid GRUB configuration file.

A16.   Answer option C is correct.

Mark will use the 'N' snag key to perform the required function. Snag keys are the single keys, which when pressed allow the system to boot from specific devices. This is the optional startup functions based on user input provided by Extensible Firmware Interface (EFI) in Mac OS X. Description of the "snag keys" are as follows:

- When 'C' key is pressed from keyboard, EFI will attempt to boot from the CD/DVD-ROM drive.

- When 'D' key is pressed from keyboard, EFI will attempt to boot from the first hard disk drive.

- When 'N' key is pressed from keyboard, EFI will attempt to boot from the Network Interface Controller (NIC).

- When 'Z' key is pressed from keyboard, EFI will attempt to boot from the ZIP drive.

Answer options A, B, and D are incorrect. All these snag keys are not used.

A17.   Answer option B is correct.

The Berkeley Software Distribution (BSD) portion of the kernel provides the primary system program interface, the Unix process model atop Mach tasks, basic security policies, user and group ids, permissions, the network stack, the virtual file system code (including a file system independent journaling layer), Network File System (NFS), cryptographic framework, UNIX System V inter-process communication (IPC), Audit subsystem, Mandatory Access Control and some of the locking primitives. The BSD code present in XNU came from the FreeBSD kernel. Although much of it has been significantly modified, code sharing still occurs between Apple and the FreeBSD Project.

Answer option A is incorrect. Mach is the core of the XNU kernel. It was originally conceived as a simple microkernel. As such, it is able to run the core of an operating system as separated processes, which allows a great flexibility, but this often reduced performance because of time consuming kernel/user mode context switches and overhead stemming from mapping or copying messages between the address spaces of the microkernel and that of the service daemons. With Mac OS X, the designers have attempted to streamline certain tasks and thus BSD functionalities were built into the core with Mach.

Mach provides kernel threads, processes, pre-emptive multitasking, message-passing, protected memory, virtual memory management, very soft real-time support, kernel debugging support, and console I/O. The Mach component also allows the OS to host binaries for multiple distinct CPU architectures within a single file due to its use of the Mach-O binary format.

Answer option C is incorrect. I/O Toolkit is the device driver framework, written in a subset of C++. Using its object-oriented design, features common to any class of driver are provided within the framework itself, helping device drivers be written more quickly and using less code. The I/O Toolkit is multi-threaded, Symmetric multiprocessing (SMP)-safe, and allows for hot pluggable devices and automatic, dynamic device configuration. Many drivers can be written to run from user-space, which further enhances the stability of the system; if a user-space driver crashes, it will not crash the kernel. However, if a kernel-space driver crashes it will crash the kernel. Examples of kernel-space drivers include Parallels, EyeTV and the Apple USB driver.

Answer option D is incorrect. The LIBKERN is the collection and container of the classes, which offers powerful services to drivers to configure its runtime environment. The LIBKERN classes offer numerous advantages, such as object introspection, and encapsulation. The LIBKERN container and collection classes closely resemble to the Core Foundation classes in name and behavior. This provides the system to automatically translate between LIBKERN and Core Foundation classes of the same type.

A18.   Answer option B is correct.

Messen Pass is application software present in Helix Live for Windows. This software allows the recovery of passwords from numerous instant messenger programs, which are as follows:

- MSN Messenger

- Windows Live Messenger

- Yahoo Messenger

- Google Talk

- AOL Instant Messenger

- Trillian Astra

- MySpace IM

Messen Pass recovers both user name and passwords and save it to HTML or text files. It can only be used to recover the passwords for the current logged-on user on local computer.

Answer option A is incorrect. Mail PassView is a password recovery tool present in a Helix Live, which is used to reveal the passwords and other account details of various email clients, which are as follows:

- Outlook Express

- Windows Live Mail

- IncrediMail

- Eudora

- Mozilla Thunderbird

- Yahoo! Mail

- Hotmail/MSN mail

- Gmail

Mail passView displays the following fields for a particular email account: Account Name, Application, Email, Server, Server Type (POP3/IMAP/SMTP), User Name, and the Password.

Answer option C is incorrect. Asterisk logger is used to reveal the passwords stored behind the asterisks in standard password text box. Asterisk Logger also displays the additional information about the revealed password: The date/time that the password was revealed, the name of the application that contains the revealed password box, and the executable file of the application etc. Asterisk Logger also provides option for saving revealed passwords in HTML and text files.

Answer option D is incorrect. Access Pass View is an application available in Windows Live side of the Helix. This application is used to reveal the database password of the password-protected MDB files, which are created by Microsoft Access or Jet Database Engine. In Access 2000/XP files, this utility cannot recover passwords that contains more than 18 characters. Access Pass View utility shows only the main database password. It cannot recover the user-level passwords.

A19. Answer option D is correct.

Trinity is using MD5 Checksum Verifier. MD5 Checksum Verifier is an application, which is used as a file integrity checker. It uses MD5 algorithm to produce cryptographic hashes. MD5 Checksum Verifier creates checksums of files and verifies their integrity. This process involves two steps:

- Create the check file.
- Verify the check file.

Answer option A is incorrect. Chaos MD5 is a generator for Windows. It takes any file as an input and generates a MD5 checksum for that file, i.e., it generates a unique signature for each and every file. Chaos MD5 does not require installation. It works just by copying it to the hard drive or USB device to run. The MD5 checksum that is generated can be used for file identification or integrity checks.

Answer option B is incorrect. Mat-MD5 is a free software, which generates MD5 hashes to check the MD5 value for each file processed and compare it with other MD5 strings. It will process one or more file and add the result value to a list. MD5 values can be compared by typing it or by copying it from an external file; this will easily compare both the values.

Answer option C is incorrect. The Secure Hash Signature Generator is an application software, which generates hash signatures that are unique to the data stored on a disk drive. These signatures are used to verify data integrity by detecting intentional or accidental tampering of drive data. The Secure Hash Signature Generator has the ability to detect up to three P-ATA, S-ATA, SCSI or ATA compatible flash devices, attached to a PC. It uses three different hash signature generating algorithms, including MD5 (128-bit signature), SHA1 (160-bit signature), and CRC32 (32-bit signature).

A20. Answer option A is correct.

John will use the chmod 764 command to accomplish the task. The command for file and folder permissions is chmod, and the proper setting according to the scenario is 764.

Answer options B, C, and D are incorrect. The chmod 777 command will provide All Access permissions to all users. The chmod 712 command will provide All Access permissions to the owner, Execute permissions to group users, and Write permissions to other users. The chmod 765 command will provide All Access permissions to the owner, Read and Write permissions to group users, and Read and Execute permissions to other users.

A21. Answer option D is correct.

"Pslist -d" command will show the statistics for all active threads on the system, grouping these threads with their owning process. Pslist is a command, which is used to display process, CPU, and memory information or thread statistics for all processes that are running presently on the system. The information listed for each process includes the following:

- The time the process has executed

- The amount of time the process has executed in kernel

- The amount of physical memory that the OS has assigned to the process

Command-line switches allows the user to view the memory-oriented process information, thread statistics, or all three types of data. These command-line switches are as follows:

-d It shows statistics for all active threads on the system, grouping threads with their owning process.

-m It shows memory-oriented information for each process, rather than the default of CPU-oriented information.

-x It shows CPU, memory, and thread information for each of the processes specified.

-t It shows the tree of processes.

Answer options A, B, and C are incorrect. All these are not valid switches.

A22. Answer option C is correct.

Fport is a tool that is used to identify unknown open ports and their associated applications. It reports all open TCP/IP applications and maps them to the owning application. It not only shows the open ports and their status but also maps them to the running processes with their PID, process name, and path. Fport contains the following five switches:

Switch Description

/?   It shows help.

/a   It sorts the result by the application.

/p   It sorts the result by the port.

/i   It sorts the result by pid.

/ap   It sorts the result by the application's path.

Answer option A is incorrect. PsLoggedOn is an applet that displays both the local and remote logged on users. If an attacker specifies a user name instead of a computer, PsLoggedOn searches the computers in the network and tells whether the user is currently logged on or not. The command syntax for PsLoggedOn is as follows:

psloggedon [-] [-l] [-x] [\\computername | username]

Parameter   Description

\-   It displays the supported options and the units of measurement used for output values.

-l   It shows only local logons instead of both local and network resource logons.

-x   It does not show logon times.

\\computername   It specifies the name of the computer for which to list logon information.

username   If an attacker specifies a user name, PsLoggedOn searches the network of computers on which the user is logged on.

Answer option B is incorrect. Pslist is a command, which is used to display process, CPU, and memory information or thread statistics for all processes that are running presently on the system. The information listed for each process includes the following:

- The time the process has executed

- The amount of time the process has executed in kernel

- The amount of physical memory that the OS has assigned to the process

Command-line switches allows the user to view the memory-oriented process information, thread statistics, or all three types of data. These command-line switches are as follows:

-d   It shows statistics for all active threads on the system, grouping threads with their owning process.

-m   It shows memory-oriented information for each process, rather than the default of CPU-oriented information.

-x   It shows CPU, memory, and thread information for each of the processes specified.

-t   It shows the tree of processes.

Answer option D is incorrect. The ping command-line utility is used to test connectivity with a host on a TCP/IP-based network. This is achieved by sending out a series of packets to a specified destination host. On receiving the packets, the destination host responds with a series of replies. These replies can be used to determine whether or not the network is working properly.

A23. Answer option B is correct.

Word Extractor is an application, which is used to extract human understandable interpretation from the binary computer files. Word Extractor tool can be used with any file present in the computer. It separates the strings that contain human text / words from binary code (like applications, DLLs). Features of Word Extractor are as follows:

- It replaces non-understandable words with spaces or dots for better understanding.

- It supports drag and drop and wrap text.

- It saves results in a TXT or RTF format.

- It does not thwart registry or system with unwanted DLL files.

Answer option A is incorrect. Forensic Acquisition Utilities (FAU) is an Incident Response tool, which is used to make image of the system's memory and any devices attached to the system. FAU contained a modified Windows version of the Unix utility dd that could image not only the hard drives but also memory. With the help of Forensic Acquisition Utilities (FAU), forensic investigators can use the search tools to find text in the memory image, IP addresses, URLs and passwords.

Answer option C is incorrect. Galleta is an application, which is used to examine the contents of the cookie files. Galleta parses the information in a Cookie file and output the results in a field delimited manner so that it may be imported into spreadsheet program. Galleta is built to work on various platforms and will execute on Windows (through Cygwin), Mac OS X, and Linux.

Answer option D is incorrect. The Forensic Toolkit Imager (FTK Imager) is a commercial forensic imaging software package distributed by AccessData. FTK Imager supports storage of disk images in EnCase's or SMART's file format, as well as in raw (dd) format. With Isobuster technology built in, FTK Imager Images CD's to an ISO/CUE file combination. This also includes multi and open session CDs. FTK imager acquires physical device images from FAT, NTFS, EXT 2, EXT 3, HFS, and HFS+ file systems.

A24. Answer options A, B, C, and D are correct.

Every virus cannot be detected by a signature-based antivirus largely for the following reasons:

- If an attacker has changed the signature of a virus, any signature-based antivirus will not be able to find the virus.

- Any new virus will not be captured by the antivirus, as it will not be on the list in the antivirus database.

- If the virus is not in the database of a signature-based antivirus, it will be virtually impossible for the antivirus to detect that virus.

- If the mutation engine of a polymorphic virus is generating a new encrypted code, this changes the signature of the virus. Therefore, polymorphic viruses cannot be detected by a signature-based antivirus.

A25. Answer options A is correct.

Virus hoaxes are false reports about non-existent viruses. In these reports the writer of virus hoaxes often claims to do impossible things. Due to these false reports the network administrator shuts down his network, this in turn affects the work of the company. These virus hoaxes falsely claim to describe an extremely dangerous virus, and declare that the report is issued by a reputed company.

Answer option B is incorrect. Chain letters are emails that urge the recipient to forward these emails to other people. Forwarding chain letters wastes the network bandwidth and user's time. Amy Bruce, Angels Exist, Applebees Gift

Certificate, ATM Theft, Bill Gates, and Bill Gates Fortune are some good examples of chain letters.

Answer option C is incorrect. Spambot is a software program that collects email addresses of users and creates a mailing list. Spam will be sent to the email addresses stored in the mailing list.

Answer option D is incorrect. Time bombs, a subclass of the logic bombs, are programs that execute at the time set by the attacker. Every time when the infected application runs, time bomb checks the date and time of the system. If the date and time of the system matches with the set time, the time bomb executes and infects the system.

Answer option E is incorrect. Logic bombs are the programs that infect a system when the predefined conditions, set by an attacker, match with the system conditions. For example, the attacker has set the execution when the video mode is set. Afterwards, the logic bomb executes when it finds that the video mode has already been set.

A26. Answer option A is correct.

In the TCP FTP proxy (bounce attack) scanning, a scanner connects to an FTP server and requests that server to start data transfer to the third system. Now, the scanner uses the PORT FTP command to declare whether or not the data transfer process is listening to the target system at the certain port number. Then the scanner uses LIST FTP command to list the current directory. This result is sent over the server. If the data transfer is successful, it is clear that the port is open. If the port is closed, the attacker receives the connection refused ICMP error message.

Answer option B is incorrect. Xmas Tree scanning is just the opposite of null scanning. In Xmas Tree scanning, all packets are turned on. If the target port is open, the service running on the target port discards the packets without any reply. According to RFC 793, if the port is closed, the remote system replies with the RST packet. Active monitoring of all incoming packets can help system network administrators detect an Xmas Tree scan.

Answer option C is incorrect. TCP FIN scanning is a type of stealth scanning, through which the attacker sends a

FIN packet to the target port. If the port is closed, the victim assumes that this packet was sent mistakenly by the attacker and sends the RST packet to the attacker. If the port is open, the FIN packet will be ignored and the port will drop that packet. TCP FIN scanning is useful only for identifying ports of non Windows operating system because Windows operating systems send only RST packets irrespective of whether the port is open or closed.

Answer option D is incorrect. TCP SYN scanning is also known as half-open scanning because in this a full TCP connection is never opened. The steps of TCP SYN scanning are as follows:

- The attacker sends SYN packet to the target port.

- If the port is open, the attacker receives SYN/ACK message.

- Now the attacker breaks the connection by sending an RST packet.

- If the RST packet is received, it indicates that the port is closed.

This type of scanning is hard to trace because the attacker never establishes a full 3-way handshake connection and most sites do not create a log of incomplete TCP connections.

A27. Answer option B is correct.

According to the scenario Adam will use "del /f /ah" command. This command will delete hidden and read only files. "/f" switch is used to force the deletion of read-only files and "/ah" switch is used to delete the hidden files.

Answer options A, C, and D are incorrect. All these commands are not used to perform the required task.

A28. Answer option D is correct.

According to the scenario, John is performing the Steganography technique for sending malicious data. Steganography is an art and science of hiding information by embedding harmful messages within other seemingly harmless messages. It works by replacing bits of unused data, such as graphics, sound, text, and HTML, with bits of invisible information in regular computer files. This hidden information can be in the form of plain text, cipher text, or even in the form of images.

Answer option A is incorrect. Web ripping is a technique in which the attacker copies the whole structure of a Web site to the local disk and obtains all files of the Web site. Web ripping helps an attacker to trace the loopholes of the Web site.

Answer option B is incorrect. Social engineering is the art of convincing people and making them disclose useful information such as account names and passwords. This information is further exploited by hackers to gain access to a user's computer or network. This method involves mental ability of the people to trick someone rather than their technical skills. A user should always distrust people who ask him for his account name or password, computer name, IP address, employee ID, or other information that can be misused.

Answer option C is incorrect. John is not performing email spoofing. In email spoofing, an attacker sends emails after writing another person's mailing address in the from field of the email id.

A29. Answer options A and B are correct.

Image hide and Snow.exe are steganography tools.

Image hide is a steganography program that hides text within an image. Steganography can encrypt or decrypt malicious data into images that appear identical to the original images. It is estimated that a 640 x 480 pixel image with a color resolution of 256 colors can hide approximately 300KB of information. High resolution images are noted for their payload. For example, a 1024 x 768 pixel image with a 24-bit color resolution can carry about 2.3MB as payload. Image hide warns its users not to save the image file in JPEG format since it is a lossy algorithm and malicious data may be lost during compression.

Snow.exe is a Steganography tool that is used to hide secret data in text files. It is based on the concept that spaces and tabs are generally not visible in text viewers and therefore a message can be effectively hidden without affecting the text's visual representation for the casual observer. It achieves this by appending white spaces to the ends of lines in ASCII text.

Answer option C is incorrect. Stegbreak is a tool that is used to detect whether steganography is performed on the suspected file or not.

Answer option D is incorrect. Anti-x is a component of Cisco Adaptive Security Appliance (ASA). Anti-x provides in-depth security design that prevents various types of problems such as viruses. The security provided by the tool includes the following:

- Anti-virus: It scans network traffic and prevents the transmission of known viruses. It detects viruses through their virus signatures.

- Anti-spyware: It scans network traffic and prevents the transmission of spyware programs. As spyware does a lot of damage, this tool becomes very critical for any organization. Spyware eats a lot of precious bandwidth too.

- Anti-spam: It deletes and segregates all junk e-mails before forwarding them to the users. It examines all e-mails that arrive in the network.

- Anti-phishing: It prevents the phishing attacks from reaching the network users.

- URL filtering: It filters Web traffic based on URL to prevent users from connecting to inappropriate sites.

- E-mail filtering: Apart from providing anti-spamming feature, it also filters e-mails containing offensive materials, potentially protecting an organization from lawsuits.

Cisco ASA appliance can be configured for network-based role for all functions of Anti-x.

A30.   Answer option B is correct.

Snow.exe is a Steganography tool that is used to hide secret data in text files. It is based on the concept that spaces and tabs are generally not visible in text viewers and therefore a message can be effectively hidden without affecting the text's visual representation for the casual observer. It achieves this by appending white spaces to the ends of lines in ASCII text.

Answer option A is incorrect. Image hide is a steganography program that hides text within an image. Steganography can encrypt or decrypt malicious data into images that appear identical to the original images. It is estimated that a 640 x 480 pixel image with a color resolution of 256 colors can hide approximately 300KB of information. High resolution images are noted for their payload. For example, a 1024 x 768 pixel image with a 24-bit color resolution can carry about 2.3MB as payload. Image hide warns its users not to save the image file in JPEG format since it is a lossy algorithm and malicious data may be lost during compression..

Answer option C is incorrect. Security Auditor's Research Assistant (SARA) is a third generation Unix-based security analysis tool that supports the FBI Top 20 Consensus on Security. It is an upgrade of the SATAN tool and operates on most UNIX platforms. SARA interfaces with NMAP for OS fingerprinting. The main features of SARA are as follows:

- It is integrated with National Vulnerability Database.

- It supports CVE standards.

- It performs SQL injection tests.

- It is available as a free-use open SATAN-oriented license.

Answer option D is incorrect. Fpipe is a source port forwarder and redirector tool. It can create a TCP or UDP stream with a source port. This tool is useful for finding out the flaws in firewalls that allow traffic through source ports to connect with internal servers. Fpipe works in the same way as Datapipe but is designed to work for Windows operating systems rather than Linux operating systems. For example, if an attacker wants to redirect the TCP port number 80 with the UDP port number 40, the attacker will use the following command:

fpipe -l 80 -r 40 -u destination_IP_addr

A31.   Answer options A, B, and C are correct.

Sam Spade, WsPingPro, or SuperScan can be used to perform a whois query. Although SuperScan works as a port scanner, it has a built-in feature to perform a whois query.

Answer option D is incorrect. Traceroute is a route-tracing utility that displays the path an IP packet takes to reach its destination. It uses Internet Control Message Protocol (ICMP) echo packets to display the Fully Qualified Domain Name (FQDN) and the IP address of each gateway along the route to the remote host. Traceroute sends out a packet to the destination computer with the TTL field value of 1. When the first router in the path receives the packet, it decrements the TTL value by 1. If the TTL value is zero, it discards the packet and sends a message back to the originating host to inform it that the packet has been discarded. Traceroute records the IP address and DNS name of that router, and sends another packet with a TTL value of 2. This packet goes through the first router, and then times out at the next router in the path. The second router also sends an error message back to the originating host. Now, the process starts once again and traceroute continues to send data packets with incremented TTL values until a packet finally reaches the target host, or until it decides that the host is unreachable. In the whole process, traceroute also records the time taken for a round trip for each packet at each router.

A32.   Answer option A is correct.

Dskprobe is a tool that is used to detect steganography. Steganography is an art and science of hiding information by embedding harmful messages within other seemingly harmless messages. It works by replacing bits of unused data, such as graphics, sound, text, and HTML, with bits of invisible information in regular computer files. This hidden information can be in the form of plain text, cipher text, or even in the form of images.

Answer options B, C, and D are incorrect. The Snow, Blindside, and ImageHide tools are used to perform steganography.

A33.   Answer options A, B, and C are correct.

Routers are hardware or software devices that are used to route data from a local area network to a different network. Routers are responsible for making decisions about which of several paths network traffic will follow to transfer the data packets. If more than one path is available to transmit data, the router determines which path is the best path to route the information. Routers also act as protocol translators and bind dissimilar networks. Routers limit physical broadcast traffic, as they operate at layer 3 (Network layer) of the OSI reference model. Routers also organize addresses into classes, which are used to determine how to move packets from one network to another. Routers ensure communication between devices on different network segments by forwarding packets between network segments.

Answer option D is incorrect. Routers limit physical broadcast traffic.

A34.   Answer option B is correct.

Frequency is not included in the routing table. The routing table consists of the following types of information:

1. Bandwidth
2. Cost
3. Delay
4. Distance
5. Load
6. Reliability

Answer options A, C, and D are incorrect. All these are included in the routing table.

A35.   Answer option A and C are correct.

Ping and TRACERT tools are used to determine the hop counts of an IP packet.The ping command-line utility is used to test connectivity with a host on a TCP/IP-based network. This is achieved by sending out a series of packets to a specified destination host. On receiving the packets, the destination host responds with a series of replies. These replies can be used to determine whether or not the network is working properly.

TRACERT utility is used to trace the path taken by TCP/IP packets to a remote computer. It traces and reports each router or gateway crossed by a TCP/IP packet on its way to the remote host. The TRACERT utility can be used with the target computer's name or IP address. It is used to detect and resolve network connection problems.

Answer Answer option B is incorrect. The netstat command displays protocol-related statistics and the state of current TCP/IP connections. It is used to get information about the open connections on a computer, incoming and outgoing data, as well as the ports of remote computers to which the computer is connected. The netstat command gets all this networking information by reading the kernel routing tables in the memory.

Answer option D is incorrect. IPCONFIG is a command-line utility that displays the current TCP/IP configuration, such as IP address, subnet mask, default gateway etc., of a networked computer. It refreshes Dynamic Host Configuration Protocol (DHCP) and Domain Name System (DNS) settings. Users can run IPCONFIG from the command prompt whenever they need to know the status of a computer's TCP/IP configuration.

A36. Answer options A, B, and D are correct.

A Sequence++ attack creates an unstable network. It could contribute to a DoS condition. The hacker continually injects a larger LSA sequence number, which indicates to the network that it has a fresher route. The original router corrects this LSA sequence number in the process known as "fight back" by sending its own LSA with a newer sequence number than the hackers sequence number.

The Max Age attack causes network confusion. It may contribute to a DoS condition. The maximum age of a LSA is 3600 seconds (one hour). Hacker sends LSA packets with maxage set. The original router that sent this LSA then corrects the sudden change in age by generating a refresh message. This process is known as "fight-back". Hacker continually interjects packets with the maxage value for a given routing value, which causes network instability.

Route table poisoning is a method of quickly removing outdated routing information from other router's routing tables by changing its hop count to be unreachable (higher than the maximum number of hops allowed) and sending a routing update. When a router receives a route poisoning, it sends an update back to the router from which it received the route poisoning, this is called poison reverse. This is to ensure that all routers on a segment have received the poisoned route information.

Answer option C is incorrect. Social Engineering attack cannot be used to attack Router. Person-to-Person social engineering works on the personal level. It can be classified as follows:

- Impersonation: In the impersonation social engineering attack, an attacker pretends to be someone else, for example, the employee's friend, a repairman, or a delivery person.

- In Person Attack: In this attack, the attacker just visits the organization and collects information. To accomplish such an attack, the attacker can call a victim on the phone, or might simply walk into an office and pretend to be a client or a new worker.

- Important User Posing: In this attack, the attacker pretends to be an important member of the organization. This attack works because there is a common belief that it is not good to question authority.

- Third-Party Authorization: In this attack, the attacker t   ries to make the victim believe that he has the approval of a third party. This works because people believe that most people are good and they are being truthful about what they are saying.

A37. Answer option D is correct.

Wireshark is an open source protocol analyzer that can capture traffic in real time. Wireshark is a free packet sniffer computer application. It is used for network troubleshooting, analysis, software and communications protocol development, and education. Wireshark is very similar to tcpdump, but it has a graphical front-end, and many more information sorting and filtering options. It allows the user to see all traffic being passed over the network (usually an Ethernet network but support is being added for others) by putting the network interface into promiscuous mode.

Wireshark uses pcap to capture packets, so it can only capture the packets on the networks supported by pcap. It has the following features:

- Data can be captured "from the wire" from a live network connection or read from a file that records the already-captured packets.

- Live data can be read from a number of types of network, including Ethernet, IEEE 802.11, PPP, and loopback.

- Captured network data can be browsed via a GUI, or via the terminal (command line) version of the utility, tshark.

- Captured files can be programmatically edited or converted via command-line switches to the "editcap" program.

- Data display can be refined using a display filter.

- Plugins can be created for dissecting new protocols.

Answer option A is incorrect. Snort is an open source network intrusion prevention and detection system that operates as a network sniffer. It logs activities of the network that is matched with the predefined signatures. Signatures can be designed for a wide range of traffic, including Internet Protocol (IP), Transmission Control Protocol (TCP), User Datagram Protocol (UDP), and Internet Control Message Protocol (ICMP).

Answer option B is incorrect. NetWitness is used to analyze and monitor the network traffic and activity.

Answer option C is incorrect. Netresident is used to capture, store, analyze, and reconstructs network events and activities.

A38.   Answer options A, B, and D are correct.

Online e-mail systems such as Hotmail and Yahoo leave files containing e-mail message information on the local computer. These files are stored in a number of folders, which are as follows:

- Cookies folder
- Temp folder
- History folder
- Cache folder
- Temporary Internet Folder

Forensic tools can recover these folders for the respective e-mail clients. When folders are retrieved, e-mail files can be accessed. If the data is not readable, various tools are available to decrypt the information such as a cookie reader used with cookies.

Answer option C is incorrect. Download folder does not contain any e-mail message information.

A39. Answer options A, C, and D are correct.

Online e-mail systems such as Hotmail and Yahoo leave files containing e-mail message information on the local computer. These files are stored in a number of folders, which are as follows:

- Cookies folder
- Temp folder
- History folder
- Cache folder
- Temporary Internet Folder

Forensic tools can recover these folders for the respective e-mail clients. When folders are retrieved, e-mail files can be accessed. If the data is not readable, various tools are available to decrypt the information such as a cookie reader used with cookies.

Answer option C is incorrect. Download folder does not contain any e-mail message information.

A40. Answer options A, B, and D are correct.

The EDB database files, STM database files, checkpoint files, and the temporary files are the main concern of a professional Computer Hacking Forensic Investigator while investigating emails that are sent using a Microsoft Exchange server. Microsoft Exchange uses the Microsoft Extensible Storage Engine (ESE).

EDB and STM database files create the storage space for email. An EDB file is used to save the formatted email including the MAPI (Message Application Protocol Interface) information. The STM database file consists those files, which are not formatted using MAPI (Message Application Protocol Interface) information.

The Checkpoint files are used by Microsoft Exchange to mark the previous point where the database was last saved to the disk. The Checkpoint files help determine whether any loss of data has occurred, thus enabling the Computer Hacking Forensic Investigator to retrieve lost or deleted messages.

Microsoft exchange uses the temporary files, also known as TMP files, to store information, which is received when the server is so busy that it cannot process it immediately. RESx.logs saves the database overflow information. These temporary files are not deleted by the system and can be recovered back.

Answer option C is incorrect. Cookie is a block of data, which a Web server stores on the client computer. If no expiration date is set for the cookie, it expires when the browser closes. If the expiration date is set for a future date, the cookie will be stored on the client's disk after the session ends. If the expiration date is set for a past date, the cookie is deleted.

A41.   Answer options B and D are correct.

A user can take the following steps to stop the Spam:

- Forward a copy of the spam to the ISP to make the ISP conscious of the spam.

- Report the incident to the FTC (The U.S. Federal Trade Commission) by sending a copy of the spam message.

Answer options A is incorrect. Email or notes to the domain administrator responsible for the initiating IP address will often fail to stop the spam.

Answer options C is incorrect. Closing an email account is not a valid step to stop Spam.

A42. Answer options A, B, C, and D are correct.

The techniques to prevent DDoS attacks are as follows:

- Applying router filtering
- Blocking undesired IP addresses
- Permitting network access only to desired traffic
- Disabling unneeded network services
- Updating antivirus software regularly
- Establishing and maintaining appropriate password policies, especially for access to highly privileged accounts such as UNIX root or Microsoft Windows NT Administrator
- Limiting the amount of network bandwidth
- Using the network-ingress filtering
- Using automated network-tracing tools

    Answer option E is incorrect. Using strong passwords is an important fact since it stops an attacker to use a computer as a zombie, the LM hash holds various loopholes and drawbacks. Therefore, it is preferable to use NTLM or NTLMv2 as a countermeasure against DDoS attacks.

A43. Answer option A is correct.

Host-based intrusion detection system (HIDS) produces the false alarm because of the abnormal behavior of users and network. A host-based intrusion detection system (HIDS) is an intrusion detection system that monitors and analyses the internals of a computing system rather than the network packets on its external interfaces. A host-based Intrusion Detection System (HIDS) monitors all or parts of the dynamic behavior and the state of a computer system. HIDS look at the state of a system, its stored information, whether in RAM, in the file system, log files or elsewhere; and check that the contents of these appear as expected.

Answer options B, C, and D are incorrect. These intrusion detection systems (IDS) do not produce the false alarm.

A network intrusion detection system (NIDS) is an intrusion detection system that tries to detect malicious activity such as denial of service attacks, port scans or even attempts to crack into computers by monitoring network traffic. A NIDS reads all the incoming packets and tries to find suspicious patterns known as signatures or rules. It also tries to detect incoming shell codes in the same manner that an ordinary intrusion detection systems does.

A protocol-based intrusion detection system (PIDS) is an intrusion detection system, which is typically installed on a Web server, and is used in the monitoring and analysis of the protocol in use by the computing system. A PIDS will monitor the dynamic behavior and state of the protocol and will typically consist of a system or agent that would typically sit at the front end of a server, monitoring and analyzing the communication between a connected device and the system it is protecting. A typical use for a PIDS would be at the front end of a Web server monitoring the HTTP (or HTTPS) protocol stream.

An application protocol-based intrusion detection system (APIDS) is an intrusion detection system that focuses its monitoring and analysis on a specific application protocol or protocols in use by the computing system. An APIDS will monitor the dynamic behavior and state of the protocol and will typically consist of a system or agent that would typically sit between a process, or group of servers, monitoring and analyzing the application protocol between two connected devices. A typical place for an APIDS would be between a Web server and the database management system, monitoring the SQL protocol specific to the middleware/business logic as it interacts with the database.

A44.   Answer option A is correct.

Monitoring the computer hard disks or e-mails of employees pertains to the privacy policy of an organization.

Answer option B is incorrect. The backup policy of a company is related to the backup of its data.

Answer option C is incorrect. The network security policy is related to the security of a company's network.

Answer option D is incorrect. The user password policy is related to passwords that users provide to log on to the network.

A45.   Answer options A, B, and D are correct.

The following steps are generally followed in computer forensic examinations:

1. Acquire: In this step, the examiner gets an exact duplicate copy of the original data for investigation. The examiner leaves the original copy intact.

2. Authenticate: In this step, the investigator shows that the data is unchanged and has not been tampered.

3. Analyze: In this step, the examiner analyzes data carefully. The examiner recovers evidence by examining hard disk drives, hidden files, swap data, the Internet cache, and the Recycle bin.

Answer option C is incorrect. Encrypt is not a step followed in computer forensic examinations.

A46.   Answer option B is correct.

Dumpster diving is a term that refers to going through someone's trash to find out useful or confidential information. Dumpster divers check and separate items from commercial or residential trash to get any information they desire. This information may be used for identity theft and for breaking physical information security.

Answer option A is incorrect. Hacking is a process by which a person acquires illegal access to a computer or network through a security break or by implanting a virus on the computer or network.

Answer option C is incorrect. Spoofing is a technique that makes a transmission appear to have come from an authentic source by forging the IP address, email address, caller ID, etc. In IP spoofing, a hacker modifies packet headers by using someone else's IP address to hide his identity. However, spoofing cannot be used while surfing the Internet, chatting on-line, etc. because forging the source IP address causes the responses to be misdirected.

Answer option D is incorrect. Phishing is a type of scam that entice a user to disclose personal information such as social security number, bank account details, or credit card number. An example of phishing attack is a fraudulent e-mail that appears to come from a user's bank asking to change his online banking password. When the user clicks the link available on the e-mail, it directs him to a phishing site which replicates the original bank site. The phishing site lures the user to provide his personal information.

A47.   Answer option A is correct.

A patent is a set of exclusive rights granted to anyone who invents any new and useful machine, process, composition of matter, etc. A patent enables the inventor to legally enforce his right to exclude others from using his invention.

Answer option B is incorrect. Artistic license ensures that the modifications to a software remain in restrictive control of the Copyright Holder. Under this licensing method, if the Copyright Holder does not like the direction of the changes, he can stop the changes.

Answer option C is incorrect. Phishing is a type of scam that entice a user to disclose personal information such as social security number, bank account details, or credit card number. An example of phishing attack is a fraudulent e-mail that appears to come from a user's bank asking to change his online banking password. When the user clicks the link available on the e-mail, it directs him to a phishing site which replicates the original bank site. The phishing site lures the user to provide his personal information.

Answer option D is incorrect. Spam is a term that refers to the unsolicited e-mails sent to a large number of e-mail users. The number of such e-mails is increasing day by day, as most companies now prefer to use e-mails for promoting their products. Because of these unsolicited e-mails, legitimate e-mails take a much longer time to deliver to their destination. The attachments sent through spam may also contain viruses. However, spam can be stopped by implementing spam filters on servers and e-mail clients.

A48.   Answer option A is correct.

Sexual Predators Act is enacted in United States in 1998, which prohibits and made illegal for an Internet Service Provider (ISP) to knowingly allow child pornography to appear on Web sites. It is necessary for an ISP to notify law enforcement that a Web site is hosted on its server, which contains child pornography material. This Web site or the pornographic contents of the Web site must be removed from the server immediately.

Answer option B is incorrect. The Child Pornography Prevention Act of 1996 (CPPA) was a United States federal law to restrict child pornography on the internet, including virtual child pornography. Before 1996, Congress defined child pornography with reference to the Ferber standard. In New York v. Ferber, 458 U.S. 747 (1982), the Supreme Court held that the government could restrict the distribution of child pornography to protect children from the harm inherent in making it. The Child Pornography Prevention Act added two categories of speech to the definition of child pornography. The first prohibited "any visual depiction, including any photograph, film, video, picture, or computer or computer-generated image or picture" that "is, or appears to be, of a minor engaging in sexually explicit conduct." In Ashcroft case, the Court observed that this provision "captures a range of depictions, sometimes called 'virtual child pornography,' which include computer-generated images, as well as images produced by more traditional means." The second prohibited "any sexually explicit image that was advertised, promoted, presented, described, or distributed in such a manner that conveys the impression it depicts a minor engaging in sexually explicit conduct.

Answer option C is incorrect. The USA PATRIOT Act, commonly known as the "Patriot Act", is a statute enacted by the United States Government that President George W. Bush signed into law on October 26, 2001. The contrived acronym stands for Uniting and Strengthening America by Providing Appropriate Tools Required to Intercept and Obstruct Terrorism Act of 2001. The Act increases the ability of law enforcement agencies to search telephone, e-mail communications, medical, financial, and other records. It eases restrictions on foreign intelligence gathering within the United States and enhances the discretion of law enforcement and immigration authorities in detaining and deporting immigrants suspected of terrorism-related acts. The act also expands the definition of terrorism to include domestic terrorism, thus enlarging the number of activities to which the USA PATRIOT Act's expanded law enforcement powers can be applied.

Answer option D is incorrect. The Prosecutorial Remedies and Tools Against the Exploitation of Children Today Act (PROTECT Act) of 2003 is a United States law with the stated intent of preventing child abuse. The PROTECT Act incorporates the Truth in Domain Names Act (TDNA) of 2003 (originally two separate Bills, submitted by Senator Orrin Hatch and Congressman Mike Pence). The PROTECT Act is codified at 18 U.S.C. 2252(B)(b). This law provides mandatory life imprisonment of sex offenses against a minor if the offender has had a prior conviction of abuse against a minor with some exceptions.

A49. Answer option A is correct.

Project Safe Childhood (PSC) is a Department of Justice initiative launched in 2006 that aims to combat the proliferation of technology-facilitated sexual exploitation crimes against children. PSC coordinates efforts by various federal, state and local agencies and organizations to protect children by investigating and prosecuting online sexual predators. PSC partners include Internet Crimes Against Children (ICAC) task forces, the FBI, U.S. Postal Inspection Service, Immigration and Customs Enforcement, the U.S. Marshals Service, the National Center for Missing & Exploited Children, and state and local law enforcement officials in each U.S. Attorney's district. PSC also helps local communities to create programs and develop strategies to investigate child exploitation.

Answer option B is incorrect. Internet Crimes Against Children (ICAC) is a task-force started by the United States Department of Justice's Office of Juvenile Justice and Delinquency Prevention (OJJDP) in 1998. Its primary goals are to provide state and local law enforcement agencies the tools to prevent Internet crimes against children by encouraging multi-jurisdictional cooperation as well as educating both law enforcement agents and parents and teachers. The aims of ICAC task forces are to catch distributors of child pornography on the Internet, whether delivered on-line or solicited on-line and distributed through other channels and to catch sexual predators who solicit victims on the Internet through chat rooms, forums and other methods. Currently all fifty states participate in ICAC.

Answer option C is incorrect. Anti-Child Porn.org (ACPO) is an organization, which has members all over the world, focusing on the topics related to child exploitation, online predators, and child pornography. Its Web site provides necessary information for law enforcement to parents, and other interested organizations. It also provides software such as Reveal, which can be used to evaluate and check files on a computer for explicit or illegal contents.

Answer option D is incorrect. Innocent Images National Initiative (IINI) is an organization, which is developed by the FBI as part of its Cyber Crimes program. This organization is established for the purpose of identifying, investigating, and prosecuting people who use computers for sexual exploitation of children and child pornography.

While performing these tasks, IINI also try to identify and release children being exploited.

A50.   Answer option A is correct.

Child Exploitation Tracking System (CETS) is a software based solution that aids law enforcement in managing and linking cases related to child protection. CETS was developed in collaboration with law enforcement. Administered by the loose partnership of Microsoft and law enforcement agencies, CETS offers law enforcement unique tools to gather and share evidence and information so they can identify, prevent and punish those who commit crimes against children.

Answer option B is incorrect. iProtectYou is a software, which is used for parental control and filtering. It controls what people, on a computer, accessing over the Internet. This tool can specify the access permission to users and groups on a computer. This tool also specifies words or phrases that will determine whether an email, Instant Message, Web site is blocked. It also block other sites that falls into specific categories, such as pornography, violence, etc. Certain newsgroups can also be blocked if they are not included in the database of child-safe groups.

Answer option C is incorrect. Reveal is an application that is used to identify objectionable material on hard disks and other storage media. This application is designed for parents to scan files on a computer containing certain keywords. This application compiles a list of multimedia files and generates thumbnails of any images on the storage media. By reviewing the report created at the end, it can be determined whether or not the files are illegal.

Answer option D is incorrect. Anti-Child Porn.org (ACPO) is an organization, which has members all over the world, focusing on the topics related to child exploitation, online predators, and child pornography. Its Web site provides necessary information for law enforcement to parents, and other interested organizations. It also provides software such as Reveal, which can be used to evaluate and check files on a computer for explicit or illegal contents.

A51. Answer option A is correct.

Quid pro quo sexual harassment is a type of sexual harassment in which a person is offered some kind of profit in exchange for sexual favors. In this type of harassment, a person can be offered a job, salary increase, promotion, etc. for sexual favors.

Answer option B is incorrect. In hostile environment sexual harassment, unpleasant or offensive environment is created in a working place. This type sexual harassment is determined on the basis of whether a reasonable person is considering the work place to be hostile or not.

Answer options C and D are incorrect. All these options are not valid types of sexual harassment.

A52. Answer options A, B, and C are correct.

When any incident of sexual harassment occurs, it is necessary that the records are maintained about the incident. Data included in this documents are as follows:

- Date and time of incident

- Location of each incident

- Names of the victims

- Details of the incident

A53. Answer option A is correct.

Unit control functions are used to review the different logs present in BlackBerry. These logs are not accessed by the standard user interface. Different unit control functions are as follows:

- Mobitex2 Radio status: This unit control function provides information about four logs, which are as follows:

- Radio status: This log helps to enumerate the state of the radio functions of the device.

- Roam & Radio: This log has a buffer of maximum 16 entries. It records information related to the tower, channel, etc.

- Transmit/Receive: This log is used to record gateway information and the type and size of data transmitted.

- Profile String: This log comprises the information of the negotiation with the last utilized radio tower.

- Device status: This unit control function provides information about different devices, port status etc.

- Battery Status: This unit control function provides information about battery type, battery load, battery status, and temperature.

- Free Mem: This unit control function provides information about memory allocation and the largest free blocks.

- WatchPuppy: This unit control function logs an entry when certain application uses the CPU after predetermined threshold and kills the processes that do not release the CPU.

A54. Answer option B is correct.

For extensive analysis of the iPod, the Mac OS is preferred over Windows and other operating systems, because iPod have better interaction with the host machine running on Mac OS. When iPod is connected to a host machine running on Mac OS, it is formatted using Apple HFS+ file system. When it is connected using a host machine running on Windows operating system, it is formatted with FAT32 file system. The Apple HFS+ file system format provides more detailed meta-data, which gives the forensic investigator extensive and elaborated information than is supplied by the Windows FAT32 file system format. An iPod connected to a machine running on Mac OS provides more meta-data for analysis.

A55. Answer option B is correct.

Jason will install iPodLinux. iPodLinux is a Clinux-based Linux distribution targeted specifically to run on Apple Inc.'s iPod. When the iPodLinux kernel is booted it takes the place of Apple's iPod operating system and automatically loads Podzilla. Podzilla is an alternative GUI and launcher for a number of additional included programs such as a video player, an image viewer, a command line shell, games, emulators for video game consoles, programming demos, and other experimental unfinished software. Many games, such as TuxChess, Bluecube, Chopper, StepMania, Doom, and Doom II can be played using iPodLinux. Recording through audio jack is at much higher quality in iPodLinux than Apple's firmware.

Answer options A, C, and D are incorrect. All these options are not valid.

Acronyms

ECOA	Equal Credit Opportunity Act
ECPA	Electronic Communications Privacy Act
EFS	Encrypting File System
exFAT	Extended File Allocation Table
FCRA	Fair Credit Reporting Act
HIDS	Host-based intrusion detection system
IDS	Intrusion Detection System
JFS	Journaled File System
MBR	Master Boot Sector
MFT	Master File Table
NIDS	Network intrusion detection system
PIDS	Protocol-based intrusion detection system
RAID	Redundant Array of Inexpensive Disks
IP	Internet Protocol
TCP	Transmission Control Protocol

UDP	User Datagram Protocol
ICMP	Internet Control Message Protocol
UDF	Universal Disk Format

Glossary

Argus

Argus is a systems and network monitoring application. It is designed to monitor the status of network services, servers, and other network hardware. It will send alerts when it detects problems.

Buffer-overflow attack

A buffer-overflow attack is performed when a hacker fills a field, typically an address bar, with more characters than it can accommodate. The excess characters can be run as executable code, effectively giving the hacker control of the computer and overriding any security measures set.

Connection hijacking

Connection hijacking is an attack when a malicious party intercepts a communication between two hosts to control the flow of communication and to eliminate the information sent by one of the original participants without their knowledge.

Cookie

A cookie is a block of data stored on a client computer by a Web server. If no expiration date is set for a cookie, the cookie expires when the browser is closed.

Cyber Law

Cyber law is a very wide term, which wraps up the legal issue related to the use of communicative, transactional and distributive aspect of networked information device and technologies. It is commonly known as INTERNET LAW.

Cyberstalking

Cyberstalking is the use of the Internet or other electronic means to stalk someone. It has been defined as the use of information and communications technology, particularly the Internet, by an individual or group of individuals, to harass another individual, group of individuals, or organization.

ECOA

The Equal Credit Opportunity Act (ECOA) is a United States law (codified at 15 U.S.C. 1691 et seq.), enacted in 1974, that makes it unlawful for any creditor to discriminate against any applicant, with respect to any aspect of a credit transaction, on the basis of race, color, religion, national origin, sex, marital status, or age; to the fact that all or part of the applicant's income derives from a public assistance program; or to the fact that the applicant has in good faith exercised any right under the Consumer Credit Protection Act.

ECPA

The Electronic Communications Privacy Act of 1986 (ECPA Pub. L. 99-508, Oct. 21, 1986, 100 Stat. 1848, 18 U.S.C. 2510) was enacted by the United States Congress to extend government restrictions on wire taps from telephone calls to include transmissions of electronic data by computer.

EFS

The Encrypting File System (EFS) is a file system driver that provides file system-level encryption in Microsoft Windows operating systems.

EnCase

EnCase is a series of proprietary forensic software products produced by Guidance Software. It is used by many law enforcement agencies and corporations around the world to support civil/criminal investigations, network investigations, data compliance and electronic discovery.

Endian Firewall

The Endian Firewall is an open source Linux distribution that specializes on Routing/Firewalling and Unified Threat Management.

exFAT

exFAT (Extended File Allocation Table) is a proprietary file system suited especially for flash drives, introduced by Microsoft for embedded devices in Windows Embedded CE 6.0 and in their desktop operating system.

FCRA

The Fair Credit Reporting Act (FCRA) is an American federal law (codified at 15 U.S.C. 1681 et seq.) that regulates the collection, dissemination, and use of consumer information, including consumer credit information.

Fork bomb

The fork bomb is a form of denial-of-service attack against a computer system. A fork bomb works by creating a large number of processes very quickly in order to saturate the available space in the list of processes kept by the operating system of computers.

Galleta

Galleta is an application, which is used to examine the contents of the cookie files. Galleta parses the information in a Cookie file and output the results in a field delimited manner so that it may be imported into spreadsheet program.

HAVAL

HAVAL is a cryptographic hash function. Unlike MD5, but like most modern cryptographic hash functions, HAVAL can produce hashes of different lengths.

Helix

Helix is a live acquisition tool, which is used to collect volatile information. It presents a portable forensic environment, which provides access to many Windows based tools.

HIDS

A host-based intrusion detection system (HIDS) is an intrusion detection system that monitors and analyses the internals of a computing system rather than the network packets on its external interfaces.

Intrusion Detection Systems

An Intrusion Detection System (IDS) is used to detect unauthorized attempts at accessing and manipulating computer systems locally, through the Internet or through an intranet.

JFS

Journaled File System (JFS) is a 64-bit journaling file system created by IBM. It is available as free software under the terms of the GNU General Public License (GPL).

John the Ripper

John the Ripper is a fast password cracker available for various environments. Its primary purpose is to detect weak Unix/Linux passwords.

JPlag

JPlag is a software plagiarism detection system. It examines program structure and uses knowledge about programming language syntax to detect plagiarism across multiple source files. JPlag currently supports Java, C#, C, C++, Scheme, and natural language text.

LIBKERN

The LIBKERN is the collection and container of the classes, which offers powerful services to drivers to configure its runtime environment.

Mat-MD5

Mat-MD5 is a free software, which generates MD5 hashes to check the MD5 value for each file processed and compare it with other MD5 strings.

MBR

The Master Boot Sector (MBR) is a 512 bytes long boot sector that is the first sector of a default boot drive.

MFT

The Master File Table (MFT) is the table where information of each and every files and directory on an NTFS file system is stored.

NIDS

A network intrusion detection system (NIDS) is an intrusion detection system that tries to detect malicious activity such as denial of service attacks, port scans or even attempts to crack into computers by monitoring network traffic.

Nmap

Nmap is a free open-source utility for network exploration and security auditing. It is used to discover computers and services on a computer network, thus creating a "map" of the network. Just like many simple port scanners, Nmap is capable of discovering passive services.

Ontrack

Ontrack is a data recovery tool, which is used to recover lost and deleted data. It provides file repair capability for files in Microsoft Word and Zip format.

Ophcrack

Ophcrack is an open source program that cracks Windows passwords by using LM hashes through rainbow tables. The program includes the ability to import the hashes from a variety of formats, including dumping directly from the SAM files of Windows.

PIDS

A protocol-based intrusion detection system (PIDS) is an intrusion detection system, which is typically installed on a Web server, and is used in the monitoring and analysis of the protocol in use by the computing system.

Privacy act

The Privacy Act of 1974, 5 U.S.C. 552a, establishes a code of fair information practice that governs the collection, maintenance, use, and dissemination of personally identifiable information about individuals that is maintained in systems of records by federal agencies.

RAID

RAID is described as a redundant array of inexpensive disks. It is a technology that allows computer users to achieve high levels of storage reliability from low-cost and less reliable PC-class disk-drive components, via the technique of arranging the devices into arrays for redundancy.

Rainbow attack

The rainbow attack is the fastest method of password cracking. This method of password cracking is implemented by calculating all the possible hashes for a set of characters and then storing them in a table known as the Rainbow table.

Sniffers

A sniffer is a software tool that is used to capture any network traffic. A sniffer changes the NIC of the LAN card into promiscuous mode due to which the NIC begins to record the incoming and outgoing data traffic across the network. A sniffer attack is a passive attack because the attacker does not directly connect with the target host.

Snorts

Snort is an open source network intrusion prevention and detection system that operates as a network sniffer. It logs the activities of the network that is matched with the predefined signatures. Signatures can be designed for a wide range of traffic, including Internet Protocol (IP), Transmission Control Protocol (TCP), User Datagram Protocol (UDP), and Internet Control Message Protocol (ICMP).

Stateful firewall

A stateful firewall is a firewall that keeps track of the state of network connections (such as TCP streams, UDP communication) traveling across it.

TCPflow

TCPflow is a program, which is used to capture the data transmitted as part of TCP connections, and stores the data in a way that is convenient for protocol analysis or debugging.

Turnitin

Turnitin is an Internet-based plagiarism-detection service created by iParadigms, LLC. Institutions, typically universities and high schools, buy licenses to submit essays to the Turnitin Website, which checks the document for plagiarism.

UDF

The Universal Disk Format (UDF) is a format specification of a file system for storing files on optical media. It is an implementation of the ISO/IEC 13346 standard (also known as ECMA-167). It is considered to be a replacement for ISO 9660, and is widely used for (re)writable optical media.

Things to Practice: A Final Checklist

The 312-49 test measures an individual's ability to identify an intruder's footprints and to properly gather the necessary evidence to prosecute. Before taking the 312-49 test, you should practice the following:

- Understand Internet laws of different countries.

- Review first responder procedure and CSIRT.

- Know the functions of file system, hard disk, and digital media devices.

- Understand Windows, Linux and Macintosh boot process.

- Practice Windows forensic tools.

- Identify commands and different kits of Linux forensics.

- Identify software and hardware tools for data acquisition and duplication.

- Identify partition recovery tools and methods.

- Understand different attacks and tools of steganography.

- Know about the password cracking tools and attacks.

- Understand wireless and Web attacks.

- Use different types of DoS attacks.

- Recognize email sending-receiving System.

- Identify corporate espionage.

- Understand laws of Copyright and Trademark.

- Understand laws on sexual harassment.

- Understand laws of child pornography.

- Study features and tools for PDA forensics.

- Study features and tools for ipod forensics.

- Study working and functions of Blackberry.

- Create investigative and evidence reports.

- Recognize privacy issue involved in investigations.

- Understand forensic process and collecting evidences.

uCertify Test Prepration Software for EC-Council Exam 312-49

uCertify test preparation simulation software (PrepKit) is designed to efficiently help you pass the EC-Council Exam 312-49. Each PrepKit contains hundreds of practice questions modeled on real world scenarios. Each exam objective is covered with full explanations of key concepts and numerous study aids such as study guides, pop quizzes and flash cards help reinforce key concepts.

Installation is simple and no internet connection is required once you have installed the PrepKit. To download a free trial please visit:

Download link:

http://www.ucertify.com/exams/EC-Council/312-49.html

At the core of every uCertify Prepkit is our powerful PrepEngine that allows for a sophisticated level of customized learning. The folks at uCertify, understand that your time is important. We have created a unique blend of learning and test preparation, the foundation of which is working smarter. Years of experience has gone into the creation of detailed reference material that ensure your learning and practice questions that closely simulate real life technical problems to test your understanding of the subject. Our time tested and continuously improving methodology instantly gives you the benefit of separating the fluff from the real deal. Anticipating your needs and customizing the material to your strengths and weaknesses is at the core of our unique engine. We help you gain the skills you need not just to pass the test, but to actually use them on the job!

uCertify's Prepkits have numerous built-in Study Aids such as Flash Cards, Study Notes, Tagging and more reduce the burden of trying to determine how to sift through vast study material by providing refresher or quick reference at any time. Studies have shown this raises the confidence level of students. The student can on the fly, customize Practice tests and learning, such that the content meets their current levels of knowledge. Immediate, Gap analysis reports tell the student what they need to learn to perform better in a particular subject area. Context sensitive study material and tips help enhance a student's knowledge of a subject area, helping them truly learn the material. This helps improve student performance and productivity on the job for employees. The platform also has the capability for subject matter expertise to be captured and communicated in a consistent manner.

Top 12 features of our Award Winning Prepkits

1. Simple, intuitive, user-friendly interface

2. One click dashboard makes it easy to find what you need

3. Guided learning steps you through the process of learning and test preparation, including crucial information about the exam format and test preparation tips

4. Reference Notes and Study Guides organized according to the actual test objectives

5. Numerous study aids, including study notes, flash cards, pop Pop Quiz and more

6. Useful Technical Articles section contains information written by industry experts and How To's that help for easy look up to specific questions

7. Collaboration

8. Exhaustive practice questions and tests, starting with Diagnostic tests to determine your initial level

9. Learning and test modes

10. Customize your tests – decide how many questions, combine one or more topics of your choice, quiz yourself on a study note, increase the level of difficulty based on your performance at any point in time, even create a test based on the amount of time you have to take a test!

11. Feedback and assessment when you need it, including Gap Analysis that clearly indicate your areas of strength and weakness

12. Full length Final Practice test that closely simulates those on the certification exam to gauge your preparation level for the actual exam

Contact us

- **Fax:** 209 231 3841
- **US:** 800 796 3062
- **International:** 1 415 513 1125
- **India:** 532 244 0503
- **Sales:** sales@ucertify.com
- **Support:** support@ucertify.com

Useful Links

- **uCertify USA:** http://www.ucertify.com/
- **uCertify India:** http://www.ucertify.in/
- **Download PrepKits:** http://www.ucertify.com/download/
- **PrepEngine Features:** http://www.prepengine.com/
- **uCertify Blog:** http://www.ucertify.com/blog

Useful Links

- **uCertify – The Fastest way to IT Certification:**
  http://www.ucertify.com/

- **Wikipedia:**
  http://www.wikipedia.com/

- **EC-Council:**
  http://www.eccouncil.org/certification/computer_hacking_f
  orensic_investigator.aspx